SEVEN SUCCESSES OF SMARTER TEAMS

PART ONE: HOW TO USE SIMPLE MANAGEMENT CONSULTING SECRETS TO STRUCTURE BUSINESS ISSUES EASILY, BUILD SMARTER TEAMS, AND SEE CAREER RESULTS NOW

Dr. A. M. Monadjem

Copyright © 2013, Accompany Advisory

www.AccompanyAdvisory.com

To purchase bulk paperback copies or schedule "Seven Successes" training please email us at admin@accompanyadvisory.com. Please allow 72 hours for responses.

Seven Successes of Smarter Teams

First published in 2013 by Accompany Advisory
13 Dion Road, Sandown Estate, Strathavon, Sandton, Johannesburg
admin@AccompanyAdvisory.com • www.AccompanyAdvisory.com

ISBN-978-1482624625

DEDICATION

I dedicate this series to the executives, managers, and graduates with whom I have shared these timeless tools. I have endless gratitude for your enthusiasm, experiences, appreciation, and impact.

BACK EDUCATIONAL WORK

Thank you! Ten percent (10%) of author royalties for this book will be used to facilitate education-related socio-economic initiatives in Sub-Saharan Africa, such as the African School for Excellence. Please support such essential grassroots causes!

TABLE OF CONTENTS

SEVEN SUCCESSES SERIES PART ONE: HOW TO STRUCTURE BUSINESS ISSUES

INTRODUCTION: WHAT ARE THE SEVEN SUCCESSES?

The Seven Successes of Smarter Teams series is a result of nearly ten years of conversations, careful listening, note-taking, research and consolidation of experience, and knowledge. Used by Accompany Advisory's Executive Learning Academy, it builds top knowledge worker-focused team effectiveness skills at all levels, especially at the middle management level. Its aim is to offer you a buffet of timeless thinking tools and techniques to make you more effective individually and as a team, whether you want to have a greater impact with the finite amount of time you have available or, alternatively, to use less time to do what you currently need to accomplish.

In order, the Seven Successes, include the following elements:

One: Structure Business Issues

Two: Solve Business Problems

Three: Simplify Business Messages

Four: Suggest Business Solutions

Five: Stimulate Team Motivation

Six: Strengthen Team Capabilities

Seven: Support Team Alignment

You can benefit from the menu of techniques in each element as much as many others have!

SERIES PROLOGUE: CAN I BUILD SMARTER TEAMS MORE EASILY?

"Your past is not your potential. In any hour, you can choose to liberate the future."

- Marilyn Ferguson

Note: *This prologue is an introduction for new readers who may not be familiar with the background of this series. If you have read any of the other books in the Seven Successes series, feel free to skip ahead.*

I've spent almost ten years, particularly while working as a consultant at McKinsey & Company, grappling with what seems to me to be a most basic question: What do great consultants really do? Strangely enough, this has been quite a challenging question to answer. I've also come to realize that the answer to this question also sheds light on what some of the most successful business brains do to succeed, particularly in building the best business teams.

Love them or hate them, somehow top-tier ex-consultants are everywhere. In fact, a pseudo-fact often used in places like McKinsey & Company is that 1 in 600 of these consultants end of becoming CEOs at the biggest and fastest growing companies in the world. This is roughly 100 times more likely than Average Joe and Jill, even for those with a good educational background. These ex-consultants often come from top-tier firms such as McKinsey & Company, BCG, Bain & Company, Booz, and Deloitte. Most have grown their skills with the so-called "Big Three" top-tier strategy firms or the "Big Four" accounting firms (sometimes "Big Five")[1], with some alternatively also working with the myriad of

---

[1] The "Big Three" are often seen as McKinsey, Bain, and BCG. The current "Big Four" (sometimes Five) are combinations of Accenture, Deloitte, PWC, E&Y, and KPMG. Various spinoffs from the original "Big Five" include firms like IBM, Cap Gemini, and Bearing Point.

exceptional niche (smaller) management consultancies in this space (see slide below).

Figure 1: Vault's Top Management Consulting Ranking (by Prestige, 2012)

Who are these former top-tier consultants? One famous example is Louis V. Gerstner, Jr., who is credited with turning IBM's fortunes around in his near-decade-long tenure as its chairman and CEO despite having limited relevant industry background (he headed American Express and Nabisco at separate times before this). A second example might be Sheryl K. Sandberg, who worked at the US Treasury, then at Google, and has been COO of Facebook since 2008. She's also a board member at Disney. A third example is Clayton M. Christensen, a Harvard professor whose groundbreaking work on innovation has inspired many entrepreneurs, myself included. The first two in this nano-sample of three are McKinsey alumni, with the third being ex-BCG (confession: some small personal bias here, perhaps?).

There are a lot of ex-consultants in key positions, in "teams" both big and small. Why is this so? Is it perhaps a big conspiracy? Some readers might argue this. Could it be their business networks? McKinsey, Bain, BCG, Booz, Deloitte, etc. all give relative youngsters direct access to Fortune 500 boardrooms globally through their work, but good business teams are unforgiving of non-star performers for very long. What about extensive industry or functional knowledge? These are topics usually well covered in education systems globally with most business leaders honing such knowledge with <u>years of focused work</u>. These two core working dimensions may seem key, but in this day, most knowledge workers, particularly management consultants, seem to change industries and career paths relatively often and easily.

Peter Drucker, the quintessential business guru, gives us a clue: "My greatest strength as a consultant is to be ignorant and ask a few questions." This points to another possible explanation for the success of former consultants all across the board. So, is there another force at play?

In this series of books, we urge you to focus on a third force besides industry experience and functional expertise: the elusive and hidden "how-to" of smarter business team success. These are the simple tools and techniques drummed into almost every top-tier consultant from Day 1. Mike George, a former director at McKinsey, explicitly indicates the importance of these techniques, saying, "The problem-solving, collaborative, and teamwork skills I developed at McKinsey have been the bedrock of my success." You may even know some of these tools, but are you using them consistently? In fact, most top management consulting firms spend more than a month a year drumming basic techniques (that we will uncover) into their associate consultants. They <u>would only do that if it were a worthwhile investment</u> for the firms and the individuals involved. This is part of the reason that each year of consulting spent deliberately using consulting techniques is often equated to three to five years "in industry," particularly from a learning curve and experience gaining point of view (see slide below).

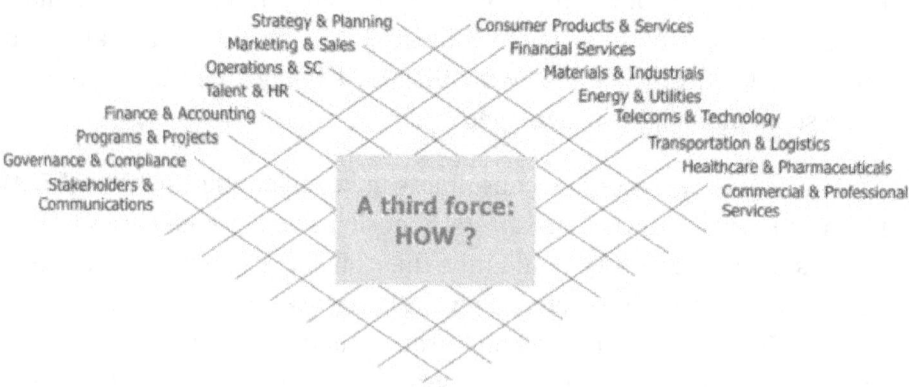

Figure 2: Functional vs. Industry Skills vs. HOW?

Looking at Vault's Prestige Ranking for Management Consulting Firms for 2012, shown earlier above, puts McKinsey & Company, BCG, and Bain & Company in its top three positions. It's no coincidence that these three firms are also consistently ranked as top three in the formal training and coaching of their staff.

Where do these tools come from? It's an open secret that many of these tools have been adapted from all sorts of professions. The best firms, businesses, and even individual free agents have "learnt how to learn," assimilating from diverse professional areas. They come from the so-called "ABLEST," which offers approaches traditionally adapted from Accounting, Banking, and Law. More recently, great thinking tools have come from other professions such as Engineering, the Sciences, such as medicine and psychology, and even from Technology-related disciplines, wherever value is found! This has created a melting pot where logical reasoning, scientific thinking, human behavior, and many other critical concepts have come together in very usable ways. As former engagement leader at McKinsey Ian Melanson has attested, "The tools you learn at McKinsey allow you to work in almost any industry that interests you and make truly significant contributions." These tools have been integrated into the Seven Successes with the aim of benefiting professionals in, as Melanson says, "almost any industry."

It's worthwhile being able to look at each of the Seven Successes in this book, and the approaches that each offers, without necessarily having to pay a few years of dues within the management consulting industry. Why go through the slog if you don't have to? But please don't misunderstand this point: While there is no substitute for experience gained through years of hard work, you can definitely fast-track your learning and impact by a few magnitudes.

You might be a middle manager, wrestling with teams and ready for career advancement. Or perhaps you're a young, new team member, hoping to excel in a great working environment. Maybe you're even an executive wanting to build a successful business team, or an external advisor helping client teams succeed. Which one relates to you the most?

Whatever your role above, there is <u>only one question that really matters</u> to achieve and maintain deep success: How do you build and maintain effective, smarter teams?

The Seven Successes of Smarter Teams allow you to have maximum impact by giving you seven interconnected elements in direct, bite-sized pieces. Each element offers a range of smart thinking tools and techniques for success (see slide below). This buffet of tools is similar to those used by many of the world's top management consulting firms.

The strength of the Seven Successes framework is the way its various elements function in tandem. According to good old Wikipedia, "Tandem is an arrangement where a team of machines, animals, or people are lined up one behind another, all facing in the same direction." This is also true for the Seven Successes, but in this case, we're talking about great business techniques and thinking tools that should be used one after the other for maximum benefit. Each of these elements has sequential and overlapping tools for solving problems. When used together, the power of the synergy becomes clear.

Figure 3: The Seven Successes of Smarter Teams

The first part of the Seven Successes meta-model works on solving a team's pressing performance problems through a series of four elements of the Business Performance Chain. The second part of the Seven Successes addresses the wider business context, or the aspects of sustainable leadership, through three core elements within the Business Health Foundation. In essence, the Seven Successes take simple, smart tools, combining them with smart, savvy teams, to unleash maximum success, both in the short and long term.

Why seven, specifically? There are already some famous "sevens" out there! We know there are Covey's seven habits, Gulick's seven functions, the seven zeros, as well as Cope's seven C's of consulting. There's even McKinsey's 7S model, in honor of which the Seven Successes are actually named (despite being a very different model!). Why not rather have, say, four or eight elements?

It is interesting to note that there are actually whole ranges of classical and cutting-edge business concepts and models up and down the number line. Below seven—there are not many one-principle systems by definition—are the two-factor theory and Board tiers. Next, there's the three C's model: change dimensions, change stages, and distinctive capabilities. Four has brand value factors, key team roles, leader styles, and types of knowledge. Five, the "helpful handful," has change factors, Porter's forces, Senge's disciplines, elements, human needs, and the 5Ws. Six has change approaches, leadership styles (different from the four!), thinking hats, and the famous sigmas.

Above seven, there are the eight management attributes: change phases, leader roles, team roles, and even an eighth missing habit! Nine raises yet a ninth habit. Ten has commandments (not the ones from Moses), schools of thought, and reinvention principles. Twelve has innovation principles, fourteen has management points, and twenty has thinking keys. As you can see, the Seven Successes model could have any number of elements. As an over-riding framework, these Seven Successes incorporate many of the ideas and techniques above into a multidimensional adaptable system that provides tried-and-true options from different schools of thought. It's up to you to remain mindful of and use the ones that work best for you. Depending on your needs, you can go a la carte and choose which aspects of the model suit your needs.

So, what problem are we solving? Whether you're a middle manager, newbie, experienced senior, or advisor, you can probably relate to the example below.

A manager in a large corporation goes into meetings constantly feeling 'fuzzy' on what he is really meant to spend time on to excel. He tries to direct his teams, but finds weeks going by without any clear idea that he is making any kind of difference whatsoever. He looks around proactively, comes across the Seven Successes, and starts sharing its techniques and concepts with his teams as a "menu" of smarter tools. He starts with techniques such as issues definition, then Logic Trees and logical reasoning, then pyramids and Abilene paradoxes. Being aware of and using these techniques makes him and his team members more aware, smarter, and faster. At all levels—seniors, peers, and subordinates—the team works more efficiently, gets far more done in far less time, and avoids needless hassles.

The Seven Successes offer the solution to the many issues and frustrations of business management. What challenges have you experienced in your work? I've observed situations like the same issues surfacing time and again, or decisions not being made, or lack of clarity on what direction to go in or what to do. Often there are famous "legacy" issues that just don't seem to disappear! Have you experienced any of these?

If the right thinking tools and techniques are used and practiced, work can also be about improvement, momentum, achievement, and action. This success can be individual, but it is all the sweeter if it's as a team, speaking the same language and getting lost, in a good way, in the collective flow of great work.

You are likely to know many of these tools and techniques. They may seem simple. However, ask yourself: do you really use them? And if so, do you use these seemingly "obvious" tools effortlessly and automatically, including doing so with your teams.

Charles Schultz's words ring particularly true at this point: "Life is like a ten-speed bike. Most of us have gears we never use." We have the potential to work as smarter teams. We just need to access it through quick, simple, and effective thinking tools and techniques. These thinking tools have personally helped many others and can bring you tremendous value in accelerating your career, whatever passion is driving you in your day-to-day work!

Dr. Ali Matthew Monadjem

Sandton, South Africa

December 2012

Before proceeding, an important note on how best to use this book: The concepts in this book, as with each one in the series, have deliberately been arranged to look first at relatively basic tools, then intermediate, then more advanced. If you are familiar with a basic concept or tool from the beginning of the section, please feel free to just scan briefly before moving on to the next section. Each level addresses roughly 1/3 of the sections, so move around as needed.

SEVEN SUCCESSES SERIES PART ONE: HOW TO STRUCTURE BUSINESS ISSUES

1   HOW DO I RESOLVE BUSINESS PROBLEMS EFFORTLESSLY?

"Think like a man of action, act like a man of thought."

- Henri Bergson

Before getting into details, the very first part of "Structuring Business Issues" is about a balance of thought and action that allows issues to be resolved and ideas to be realized. We do this by adhering to the Business Performance Chain, which we will be deconstructing all throughout this series.

First, however, let's examine a brief story to illustrate the chain's importance.

Can you relate to this?

A manager assigns a pressing business problem to an enthusiastic new team member. The team member is capable and very willing. She works diligently and tirelessly on the issue. She works day and night for six months and checks in regularly with her manager. She certainly has the deep technical expertise to tackle the issue, and she has a very good knowledge of the organization. She has always been a star in her previous roles! After six months, her suggestions are presented to her senior management, who were unwilling to implement her suggestions. Her work is criticized for being "disjointed," "sloppy," "too complex," and "not

17

actionable." Needless to say, she takes these comments personally and resigns five days later.

Why would someone fail when they had been seen as successful in all their previous roles?

To discover the reason, we turn to the quotation above: "Think like a man of action, act like a man of thought." This is the essence of the chain. The Business Performance Chain can almost be seen as the first half of the Seven Successes. It is made up of four essential elements in tandem, one after the other. In short, these are: Structure, Solve, Simplify, and Suggest. We will expand on each one in turn.

Figure 4: Seven Successes of Smarter Teams - Business Performance Chain

These tools, when used together, improve performance through identifying the most important solutions for any business problem, or business idea, in any given circumstance.

So let's get started with the first Success. "Structure Business Issues" is about setting the scene correctly up front. *Structure* is the start of a journey that has strong repercussions on the subsequent three chained elements. Nevertheless, it's often forgotten in the fray of seemingly excellent "problem solving."

Think of techniques such as objective setting, problem definition, context clarification, problem structuring, and Mind Mapping. It's about understanding business context, defining SMART goals and SMART objectives, and using Logic Trees. This is essentially about defining business issues and disaggregating these into relevant pieces for team members to manage further. Most critically, this is about understanding "what you are solving" before you rush to start solving—a surprisingly common issue and one that, if addressed, can save tremendous amounts of management time and effort from being wasted.

So what kind of questions would this Success element address? Let's raise a few: Am I aware of all the issues my team faces? What issues should we be working on now? How do I clarify an issue enough to resolve it? How do I define any problem I may face? How can I break issues into manageable pieces? How do I make sure I don't miss key facets? What are the critical elements of any issue? How do I break problems down really quickly? How do I get to the true causes of any problem? What can I do to unleash my team's creativity?

Fundamental concepts include tools such as the SLOT matrix, the 6S Issue Clarifiers, SMART Approaches, Root Cause Tools, and Logic Tree Structure. There are more, but these are the key ones. You may *know* about some of these tools, but do you actually *use* them easily and often.

Remember, if you're solving the wrong problem, even if the "answer" is great, then you're wasting everyone's precious time.

2   CAN I AVOID THE DANGER OF JUMPING TO BUSINESS CONCLUSIONS?

"To succeed, jump as quickly at opportunities as you do at conclusions."

- Benjamin Franklin

Before diving into the details of dissecting business issues, we are going to step back one more time in the next few pages. In this section, we're going to go into the importance of stepping back on the causes limiting either team or business performance and how these relate to your priority issues that are tackled day to day.

In other words: Don't jump to conclusions or causes in your business team. There is a deceptively simple tool to use to address this. You may know it, but don't let its simplicity fool you!

Here's a situation to consider for subsequent discussion.

You have been part of your company's management team for over two years now. Since then, you've worked non-stop, feverishly putting out any fires that have blazed in your area of the business. In the monthly management meeting, where work is assigned, you find that the MD raises the issue of poor staff capabilities (yet again). You can see the team around you is stretched. The team has focused on up-skilling poor performers and correcting legal loopholes in the business—in essence, addressing various aspects of high company risk. The company should be in a better position, particularly considering how hard the team has worked. Nonetheless, despite their best efforts, the team is still not likely to see better results any time soon.

2. Can I Avoid the Danger of Jumping to Business Conclusions?

Why has this been the enduring pattern? Why are results poor despite extensive effort?

In this section, we're sharing a key matrix that is often misunderstood and discussing how the matrix should be used for impact, what other tools can be overlaid with it, and how this helps a team step back smartly.

We certainly know that businesses and managers have intense frustrations. These usually get "resolved" ineffectively through constant firefighting. Why is this?

The first problem is that teams jump to conclusions in terms of both what the problem is and how to solve it. They apply standard, widely accepted common sense solutions to these problems. They think they know the answer based on previous experience and patterns. Even worse than this, though, is when teams jump to conclusions further back when trying to identify <u>real</u> causes, constraints, and issues.

How do you avoid this? Avoiding this personal bugbear unlocks massive value and time and makes life much easier, no matter whatever position you may currently be in.

One simple way to look more broadly is to use the classic SLOT Matrix. You've probably seen this a few times, but how often have you used it to build linkages for your portfolio of initiatives? Let's use it now, but not in the usual, superficial way.

To remind you, simply put, the two key dimensions of the SLOT Matrix are Internal vs. External, as well as Possibilities vs. Problems or, in other words, helpful and harmful issues in relation to business objectives (shown in the slide below).

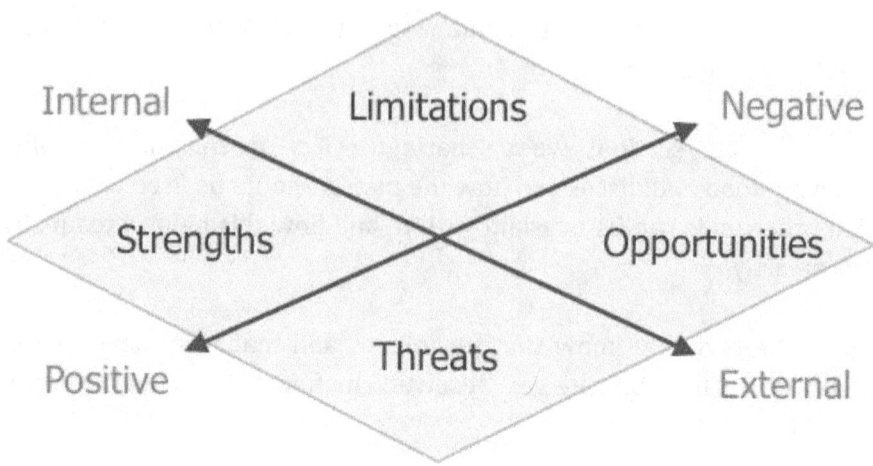

Figure 5: SLOT Matrix

The matrix has had bad press at times from being <u>misused for business objective-setting</u> where other models are actually much more useful, such as the so-called BCG matrix. But it is equally underused for issue identification.

By looking at the intersections of the two dimensions, this collection of Strengths, Limitations, Opportunities, and Threats, you can SLOT test your objectives to see if they reflect reality. Understand each of your objectives through the four lenses of the SLOT Matrix. Does your list of initiatives match the current internal reality of the business while also considering the competitive landscape it's in?

Once this is done, then make sure that "external positives" (Opportunities) are also sufficiently considered. This is often about revenue-generating potential, such as new markets, new products, and new ways of looking at existing asset configurations.

Sounds obvious, but often in the thick of it, we shut down somewhat and react instinctively with the fetal position of introverted business thinking about our given business circumstances. It's a reflection of a natural fight-or-flight response to protect your castle. This often creates a bipolar approach where teams bounce between the two extremes of the proverbial glass being half-empty, then half-full. But if you're aware of this, it really helps open up your thinking a great deal.

How do you easily create a useful SLOT Matrix? What topics should you cover? One particular way of looking at it is to overlay other useful models on a "third" dimension across each of the four corners of the Slot Matrix (beyond Internal vs. External and Possibilities vs. Problems).

For example, Kenichi Ohmae's 3C model of Company (or usually Corporation), Customer, and Competitor is one very useful overlay. In essence, you force yourself to look at your internal assets, to segment your audience, and to differentiate yourself relative to other market players.

A second way is to use McKinsey's original 7S model as that third dimension. As a reminder, this has "hard" elements of strategy, structure, and systems; and "soft" elements of skills, style, staff, and shared values.

There are others such as PESTEL: Political; Economic; Social; Technological; Environmental; Legislative/Legal. But this is usually more externally focused and often used more with consumer-facing or B2B companies.

The point is not to necessarily get hooked on and discuss any specific model in detail here—that can be done elsewhere. The point, rather, is to highlight smart ways to gain useful insights about your overall team and the possible portfolio of problems and possibilities you and your team should be paying the most attention to.

So, how can you gain insights from the SLOT Matrix? Simple.

Firstly, you can match strengths and opportunities in themes and see if there are synergies. Taking external and internal positives can be very valuable; think of Apple's simple design philosophy and innovation with market demand for sleek personal gadgets, like iPods.

Secondly, you can convert weaknesses and threats to strengths and opportunities by considering how to release current constraints and exploring new dimensions of success. For example, "cheap," or low-quality products, can become value items in new markets.

Thirdly, and this might sound bizarre, you can just choose to ignore your weaknesses and... get on with the work. This is particularly useful if there's not much you can do about the particular issue at the given time with finite resources, such as financial outlay and focused effort. For example, you may not have the marketing resource you've dreamed of to build out your product range, but instead of using such constraints as an excuse, you need to persevere and work around it with what you have. Of course, clearly some creativity is needed to understand the true nature of your constraints instead of just assuming that they are fixed and unchangeable.

In the final analysis, this approach gives a well-balanced list of ideas to be prioritized as initiatives in the team or business. It is vital to have a reasoned collection of initiatives to structure further, which we dive into a few sections further down when we discuss root cause tools and Logic Trees. Remember, GIGO: Garbage In, Garbage Out.

Before concluding this section, it's important to beware not to treat individual issues equally by default. An issue arising from a particular strength may be 10 times as critical as another. The human mind often equalizes an initiative's importance even if the magnitudes of opportunity or disaster are scales apart.

In conclusion, use the SLOT approach to anchor your business or management priorities effectively in conjunction with tools like SLOT, 3C, 7S, and PESTEL. These will help you not jump to conclusions, not just in prejudging solutions with an automatic (often incorrect) response to ideas and initiatives, but also in the formation of the portfolio of ideas, be they problems or possibilities.

This offers an alternate perspective on the projects or work packages the team should be tackling, as opposed to basing these decisions purely on raw opinion. It's impossible to be entirely objective, of course, but this way, your thinking will be far more reflective of business reality and aligned with its purpose.

Once you can do this "stepping back" across the whole horizon of issues without reacting automatically or jumping to conclusions, it becomes a lot easier to tackle the right issues at the right time, one at a time, in the interests of your sustained success.

Keep in mind the importance of stepping back on the causes limiting team or business performance and how to determine a more complete and appropriate list of priority issues.

***

Questions to consider:

What kinds of issues do you tend to firefight immediately?

How do you deal with "urgent" issues?

How do you think this affects your business success?

How could you start preventing issues?

How can you use the SLOT Matrix effectively?

3   HOW DO I MAKE SURE PRIORITY PROJECTS ARE PRECISE?

"In displaying the psychology of your characters, minute particulars are essential. God save us from vague generalizations!"

- Anton Chekhov

In this section, we're going to benefit from being SMART with business issues and share how this allows more efficient work on priority issues. The SMART Issues Approach to business issues is extremely easy to use and useful.

But first, a scenario to give us perspective:

Your team has been working together for almost six months now and your team leader has been a great person to work with so far. Right now, you're working on a report on the "strategic direction of the company's product portfolio." Your team leader asked you to do this a while back and you've reworked the report seven times now. Team members have given you vague suggestions, which you've taken into consideration. You've noticed, however, that you're starting to receive more and more contradictory suggestions. You've worked long hours, but have found that pieces of work that team members are assigned don't seem to "get done." Some have been raised in meetings for the last five months with no closure. Why? What can you do about this?

It seems George Doran first raised the SMART acronym for business, though it's often attributed to Peter Drucker. Let's see what this is about.

Business teams often go into autopilot, particularly in crisis or under duress, and start solving a problem or addressing possibilities before they even know <u>exactly</u> what problem they are solving. This is a relatively common trap to fall into, even if you're aware of this challenge.

Defining an issue clearly up front, whether that issue is a problem or possibility, is an incredibly useful, no-regret step for any business team. It can save endless amounts of time down the road suffering from misunderstandings and wasted effort.

Here is where some of Peter Drucker's work as a management guru finds a very useful home. Drucker's Managing By Objectives (MBO), first raised more than half a century ago, has over the years encouraged teams to clearly articulate the objectives of the team or even individual team members, with seniors and subordinates working together to collaboratively construct a crystal-clear understanding of what a team or individual is working on.

The SMART Issues Approach seems to have become the logical mascot of this. George Doran apparently first described this approach by acronym over 30 years ago. It's a timeless tool, still as useful today as it was then. As with the earlier two tools in this series, don't let its simplicity fool you!

There are various versions of SMART that I've experienced in the context of business and management consulting. However, it usually stands for a few well-known but under-applied rules: Specific, Measurable, Actionable, Relevant, and Timely. This is shown in the slide below.

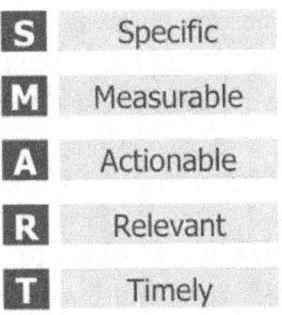

Figure 6: SMART Approach

What do we mean by this? Let's take each one in turn. It is very useful to make sure each of these points is addressed when defining a critical issue or idea you or your team are working on.

Specific is about being completely clear and unambiguous about where you're going. A specific statement should not leave much room for misinterpretation or confusion through vagueness or generality. The team must understand specifically what it must accomplish, who will do it, and, ideally, it should even be clear why it should be done. Try to leave nothing "self-evident[2]."

Key questions include: What's expected? Who's involved? Where are we doing this? Why? What's important about our goal?

Measurable is about being able to see progress towards an end state, from the "As-Is" toward the so-called 'To-Be" state. If clear steps, deliverables, or tangible outcomes are outlined, it becomes much easier to make progress and, more importantly, "feel" progress. This is particularly important to ensure expectation management with your team, superiors, and customers or clients.

Here, it's a matter of asking: How many deliverables are there? How detailed does each really need to be? What sub-elements does each have? How do these break down into discrete pieces? What are the key components? What are the relevant KPAs and KPIs?

Actionable is about choosing a goal that can be controlled through the team's skill base and efforts. It should be a stretch target from current "As-Is" performance, but not too far away or unattainable as to make it demotivating or even possibly "professionally risky" for an individual to try for or be a proactive part of. Most team members, even high

---

[2] Holding key points self-evident is often also done unconsciously with business assumptions, a point addressed further under another part of this Series in "Solve Business Problems."

performers, will hesitate (or should to some degree) if you're expecting them to be productivity kamikazes up front.

Also, there will always be external factors that play a role and influence an outcome, but make sure that what you're working on is actually feasible to do. Consider your team composition. I've found many business teams fall into the trap of perceiving that they control more elements than they actually can in reality, or they try to control the wrong levers, find something has changed, and attribute this to the action that they took. Be careful here not to take credit for the vagaries of chance (or vice versa). It might be satisfying but it is not constructive.

Relevant is making sure that, while you're efficient at getting a lot done, you're also effective in doing what should be done. In other words, don't just get busy for its own sake, but make sure you're getting busy doing what matters to your business, your entity, and your team.

This is incredibly important in the sense that many teams, particularly in large bureaucracies, tend to spend an inordinate amount of time reporting and attending meetings and training sessions. When asked how these are relevant to the goal you're trying to achieve, you may find that there are blatant mismatches. Getting busy is clearly not the same as adding real value. Try to make sure you're consciously "cutting the fat out" periodically, perhaps even doing this discretely for five minutes twice a day. For example, true story: Making sure the manager has instructed someone to swap the positions of the break room's coffee machine, microwave, and fridge by 4 PM may be great with regard to all the other elements above, but might not be incredibly relevant.

Timely is the last element. This refers to having clear time-based parameters that tell the team how soon they need to achieve their target. Does a task need to be done in the next hour, day, week, or month? Does it link to a preceding dependency or a subsequent step?

Being timely should include carefully considering the amount and ability of the human resources within the team so as not to set itself up for failure every single time. It's important to create a sense of urgency of what can be achieved in various time frames, separated from day-to-day banality. What can we achieve one week out? One month out? One quarter? Six months? One year? Five years?

In particularly ambiguous circumstances, this requires a particular depth of thinking to make sure expectations are managed carefully in the event that there are delays. This is a matter of preventing (or reducing) ridiculous over-scoping or over-promising results in double-time, especially while the team is already doing its utmost to catch up with unattainable targets.

Make sure you put your issue or idea at the heart of the smarter SMART Issues Approach. In other words, make sure it "ticks all the boxes" before you proceed to structure it any further with subsequent techniques. Remember: Specific, Measurable, Actionable, Relevant, and Timely. This is shown below for clarity.

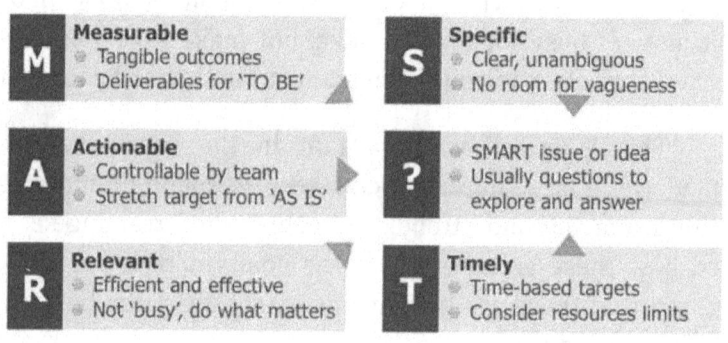

Figure 7: Smart Issues Approach Point & Smart Issue / Idea

In this section, we shared the easy-to-use SMART Issues Approach, what each aspect stands for, how each element impacts your work, and how this helps define any issue clearly.

***

Questions to consider:

What work clarification approaches have you used?

Which were or weren't successful in jumpstarting your work efforts? Why?

3. How Do I Make Sure Priority Projects are Precise?

How did it impact your work?

Does using the SMART Issues Approach highlight any deficiencies in your approach? How can these be remedied?

4   CAN I USE MY OWN SMART APPROACH?

"This idea that there is generality in the specific is of far-reaching importance."

- Douglas R. Hofstadter

As a follow-up to the core SMART Issues Approach, we're going to take time to ensure you build a personal SMART model that you can share and use day to day in your work. This is useful, as it provides a way for you to own this approach, for it to stick strongly in your mind, and hopefully for it to become a regular habit, if this is not currently the case.

In other words, you are building <u>your own SMART Issues Approach</u> to business issues. It should be extremely easy to remember and apply in vastly differing situations.

Here's a true story for our discussion:

You've heard about the term SMART before, but have not used it in your work. It's a good idea, but it has stayed conceptual to you. Team members have regularly discussed the concept and what it means to each of them. Most leave it unused, however, preferring the perception of having freer flowing creative and open debates. Using simple acronyms can seem so restrictive!

Below are a few comments you've heard in the past (sometimes whispered conspiratorially).

"Is the 'S' meant to be 'specific' or 'significant'?"

"What about 'A'? Is that 'action-oriented' or 'actionable'?"

"I've heard that the 'T' is not 'timely,' but should really be 'time-bound.'"

"I'm not sure of the exact correct model, so let's not argue."

This confusion is often interpreted to mean that the approach is not useful day to day.

In this section, we're looking at variations on the SMART Issues Model, what each aspect can stand for, how you should customize your SMART, and how this can support you day to day.

To start, a relevant principle from Elbert Hubbard: "Many people fail in life, not for lack of ability or brains or even courage, but simply because they have never organized their energies around a goal."

Your own SMART Issues Approach can help you avoid this problem.

We've previously discussed the "classical" SMART Issues Approach with it being useful to make sure issues are stated to be Specific, Measurable, Actionable, Relevant, and Timely. Hopefully, this mantra-style repetition is becoming old hat now!

Let's show an example to be clear exactly what is meant, as well as exactly what is not intended here. Let's take the statement: "Let's improve our business performance!"

OK. What does this mean exactly? Should we increase profit? Should we invest more in staff training? Should we move to better offices? Such a vague statement would need to be made much more specific.

So: Specific? No.

Measurable: There's not really anything to quantify...so, no.

Actionable: No.

Relevant: Can't tell because it's not specific enough, so by default, no.

Timely: No.

Let's try this again. For example: Team X will increase our gross revenue from product A by 10% within the next 12 months.

Specific? Yes. It talks about gross revenue increase from product A.

Measurable? You bet. Ten percent from current levels is measurable.

Actionable? It seems so. It's about team X doing the work on a single product over a short period of time.

Relevant? If it's a private company: yes. According to McKinsey's book, *The Granularity of Growth*, gross revenues are usually relevant for growth.

Timely? Yes, in the next 12 months.

Remember, the SMART Issues Approach mentioned in the last section is critical to make sure your issues are clarified individually or as a team.

Now that we have used the classic approach, it's time to turn it upside down a little. It's time to customize your own SMART Issues Approach, to personalize it depending on your style and your priorities. Over the years, the SMART elements have proliferated like a bad game of so-called Chinese whispers and produced various other useful terms and approaches.

Let's look at these now.

S. Previously Specific.

This can refer to: Simple, Structured, Significant, Stretch, or Substantive.

M. Previously Measurable.

This can refer to: Meaningful, Manageable, Monitored, or Motivating.

A. Previously Actionable.

This can refer to: Agreed, Ambitious, Appropriate, Assignable, or Achievable.

R. Previously Relevant.

This can refer to: Realistic, Results-oriented, Resonant, Resourced, or Right (correct).

T. Previously Timely.

This can refer to: Time-boxed[3], Time-bound, Timetabled, Trackable, and Tangible.

There are quite a few terms here with varied meanings. Choose your favorites and let us know what works best for you.

Which SMART Issues Approach works best for you? Later, we'll also take SMART further as SMARTER when we look at the element of suggesting actionable solutions[4].

---

[3] In this context, "time-box" refers to the idea of forcing a task or engagement to take a predetermined amount of time that is a fraction of how long it should "normally" take.

[4] This is part of Seven Successes "Suggest Business Solutions" material.

In this section, we shared variations on the SMART Issues Approach, what each aspect can stand for, how you should customize your SMART Issues Approach, and how this can support you day to day. This is a great buffet to choose from. Decide your own SMART Issues Approach and use it from today to support you in stepping back and defining issues.

***

<u>Questions to consider:</u>

What SMART Issues Approach do you favor day to day?

What are the work implications of using different terms in your approach?

5   HOW DO I DEFINE BUSINESS ISSUES CLEARLY?

"If I had an hour to save the world, I would spend 55 minutes defining the problem and 5 minutes finding solutions."

- Albert Einstein

We're now going to dive into how to set the context for each business issue you or your team faces at work on a daily basis. We will share an easy-to-use approach that is simple to apply across your business.

But first: an uncomfortable scenario.

Your current project assignment is scheduled to finish in the next four weeks. It's been a grueling three months of team effort. Your team is ready to write its project closeout report. In it, you are asked about the scope of the project, its objectives, and deliverables. A team member forwards you an email with a few notes that were taken in an introductory meeting; however, none of the points seem to address the original scope of the project. You get some advice from an experienced project manager you respect, who asks you: Did you write a project charter for your project? Did you define the problem you were solving? You don't remember your team doing that and are wondering what "defining the problem" actually really means. You wonder: Could this have been useful up front?

Bear in mind Einstein's words as the start of this section. Also, consider the following saying by Lambert M. Surhone, alluding to the usefulness of the tool in this section: "Context analysis is a method to analyze the environment in which a business operates."

In this section, we're sharing the 6S Business Issues Clarification Model, what each 'S' stands for, why these factors are important, and how this supports your issues clarification.

Our first critical step to building successful business solutions is to deconstruct each particular issue a team has identified. Each problem or possibility can now be evaluated and articulated in detail in relation to six critical dimensions.

Remember the SMART Issues Approach? Now we take the SMART issue or idea we wrote down there and look at it along 6 dimensions. In short, it's about defining the problem through the Business Issue Clarification Model. These dimensions are, in order: Setting, Stakeholders, Success (Defined), Scope (Clarified), Stoppers, and Sources. This 6-pack of dimensions is what should be kept in mind, with each issue being considered front and center, as shown below.

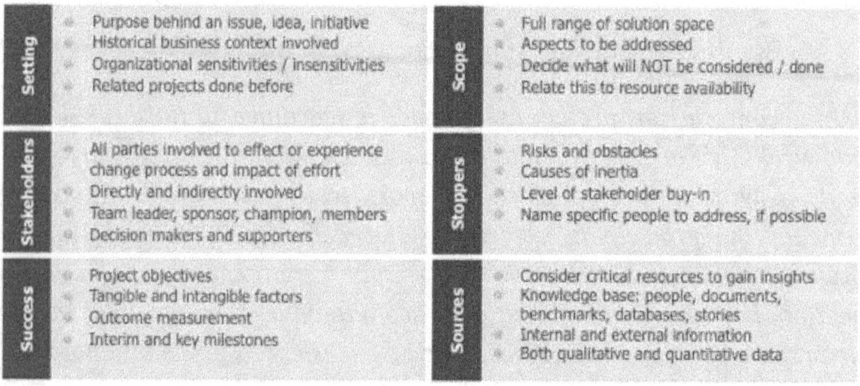

Setting	Scope
• Purpose behind an issue, idea, initiative • Historical business context involved • Organizational sensitivities / insensitivities • Related projects done before	• Full range of solution space • Aspects to be addressed • Decide what will NOT be considered / done • Relate this to resource availability
Stakeholders	**Stoppers**
• All parties involved to effect or experience change process and impact of effort • Directly and indirectly involved • Team leader, sponsor, champion, members • Decision makers and supporters	• Risks and obstacles • Causes of inertia • Level of stakeholder buy-in • Name specific people to address, if possible
Success	**Sources**
• Project objectives • Tangible and intangible factors • Outcome measurement • Interim and key milestones	• Consider critical resources to gain insights • Knowledge base: people, documents, benchmarks, databases, stories • Internal and external information • Both qualitative and quantitative data

Figure 8: Business Issues Clarification Model Key Points

Let's discuss the first one: <u>Setting</u>. This is about understanding the purpose behind addressing the issue.

What is the historical business context involved?

What has been tried before?

What is the organization sensitive or insensitive to?

Dependencies? Complexities?

How quickly does the issue need to be resolved?

How critical is it? Why is it critical?

What projects have run before, are currently running, or are planned for the future, and how do they need to be contextualized?

Let's discuss the second one: <u>Stakeholders</u>. This is about all the parties involved in the creating, building, or experiencing of the end state.

Who is directly or indirectly involved?

Who is the team leader? Sponsor? Champion? Team members?

Who are the decision-makers and influencers?

Who are senior or junior?

Who is formally powerful vs. informally so?

Who are internal vs. external parties?

Who are the beneficiaries of a solution?

Who is invested in the success or failure of the project?

Who has been part of similar or interdependent projects?

Where possible, try to choose specific people who you can engage with, rather than a vague group of stakeholders who can't be tackled practically one by one even with specific engagements (e. g. interviews). This helps with clear stakeholder management support later.

The third one is <u>Success</u>.

What are the project objectives?

How should the issue's outcome be measured?

How about "soft" or intangible success factors? For example, if company culture or skill level is important, you can later use surveys or interviews to get this measure right.

There may also be intermediary milestones to success that are important, but are often missed opportunities because a team is just thinking purely about the end-state of success. [5]

The fourth one is <u>Scope</u>.

Scope is about clearly articulating the full range of the solution space. Discuss what should be addressed. Also, discuss and clearly decide what will <u>not</u> be considered. This second aspect of scope is often more important than the first, as knowing what resources you do not have at your disposal or what solutions won't even be considered saves a lot of time and prevents problems later.

Say, for example, you need to increase sales of your product: It would be great to know up front that you do not have an option to increase the salary bill or, if you are perhaps in labor-sensitive markets, that you will not be able to fire anyone.

Although you should of course question the validity of these restrictions, knowing them up front is important to avoid going down the wrong rabbit-hole, so to speak.

Number five is <u>Stoppers</u>. Essentially, this is about barriers.

What are the risks and obstacles that should be overcome on the way toward the improved solution?

What could cause inertia?

Will there be stakeholder buy-in?

---

[5] We will discuss this more later as part of "Suggest Business Solutions."

Is there change fatigue from no-stop effort?

Again, here it's about managing the obstacles specifically.

Are there parties mentioned across the stakeholder dimension that will be particularly resistant, passively or actively so?

The sixth one: Sources. This is a consideration of the resources, usually knowledge-based, that can be relied on that improve the quality of the projects; for example, people, documents, books, websites, and databases that provide relevant answers.

What information is internal vs. external?

What is "at hand" vs. "needs to be found"? Specialists?

What about experienced leaders? Benchmarks? Stories?

Think not only of either quantitative or qualitative data—both are important. We will look into this in more detail later.

A point to note here: Organizations are notoriously bad at using their own internal data to add value to their own insight-generation process. Often, consultants come in to an entity only to make sense of a department's own data and to draw trends answers from this fertile ground.

Overall, the issues definition process is similar to what is often more formally referred to as a "project charter." This usually has similar sections, but the point often gets lost in the formal reporting process of large organizations.

Why not just use a project charter instead of the project definition process outlined above? You certainly could use a charter, as these often address points around purpose, objectives, activities, deliverables, critical success factors, stakeholders, timelines, due dates, risks, etc.

Charters are useful, but I've found that they often scare teams away through being perceived as relatively complex and "adminy." It also does not help that these are often being used relatively rigidly, formally, or bureaucratically within corporate reporting environments. In this context, charters can encourage overthinking an issue.

The aim of the Business Issue Clarification Model, or the 6S sheet, is to start as an important but relatively informal single-page anchor for the project or work package. This can then be built up on an ongoing basis. This page captures a summary of the points made previously.

This should link in with the SMART Issues Approach by taking the SMART issue or idea above and transplanting it among the 6Ses here on the left side (shown below). This can form 80% of the basis of a project charter if needed, but should also be a "living document" that is done once at high speed without too much overthinking. This can then be tested with various stakeholders, often informally and interactively, to check alignment and direction.

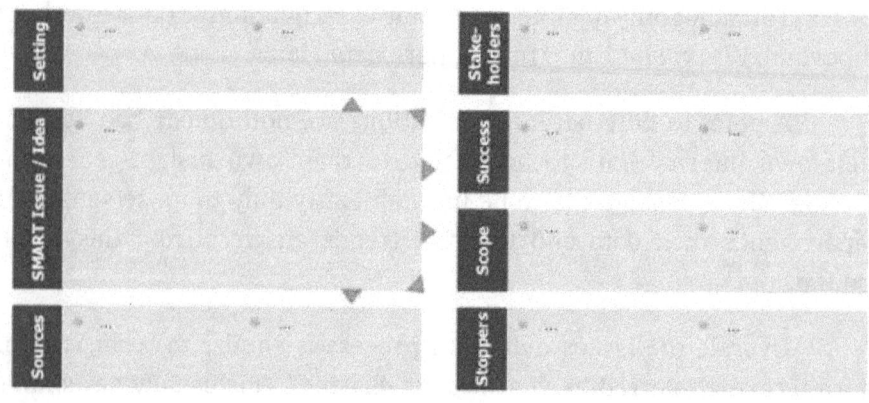

Figure 9: Combined Smart / 6S Model

In this section, we shared the 6S Business Issues Clarification Model, what each "S" stands for, why these factors are important, and how this supports your issues clarification process.

***

Questions to consider:

What part of the 6S Business Issues Clarification Model have you found most useful?

How do the 6S elements relate to each other?

What is the difference between 6S and a project charter?

What tools can you combine with 6S to effectively clarify your issues?

6   SHOULD I USE ROOT CAUSE THINKING?

"Do not look at where you fell, but where you slipped."

- African proverb

We're now going to clarify root cause thinking and what it can do for you.

But first, here's a scenario relevant to this section, based on a true story:

You've been promoted to a shift manager position at a production site. It's hard work, but you even get danger pay. You notice the shift workers leaving their posts early, usually 30 minutes, but sometimes up to an hour. The problem seems to have gotten worse as the operations expand to more people, and it's affecting production significantly. Your boss gives his perspective clearly: "It's a matter of basic discipline. You're letting a culture of 'devil-may-care' emerge here, and you'd better nip it in the bud quickly to avoid laziness issues in the future!" You schedule a meeting with your staff and are ready to go in guns blazing. You're convinced that you will turn the tide quickly like this.

What is the root of the issue here? Can you guess? You'll be surprised at the answer, which is given in the next section.

In this section, we're going to define what Root Cause Thinking is, clarify the difference between symptoms and roots, specify when you should use Root Cause Thinking, and demonstrate how this can give you the edge in your business team.

But first think of the quotation at the top of the section, an old African proverb: "Do not look at where you fell, but where you slipped." This is a relevant thought, as we'll see below.

So let's consider another problem. Do you share this common experience with colleagues?

An associate comes to his or her manager with a pressing problem, seeking guidance and, hopefully, a solution. The manager responds by asking a few questions, normally limited to the scope of the problem and its effect on the task at hand. The manager, practiced in this kind of reactive problem-solving, suggests a creative and practical work process to minimize or eliminate the problem's negative effects. The associate implements the solution as directed and work continues.

This scenario is played out daily in most organizations. On the surface, this type of problem solving is effective and practical. In fact, managers are often rewarded for their ability to keep work flowing on schedule regardless of challenges and obstacles. Why, then, do legacy problems and issues continue to reappear constantly?

The answer to this question is simple. Traditional problem-solving addresses symptoms and overcomes them, much like a bad doctor. It does not consider what's under the surface or look at WFB, in other words: What's Floating Beneath (see below).

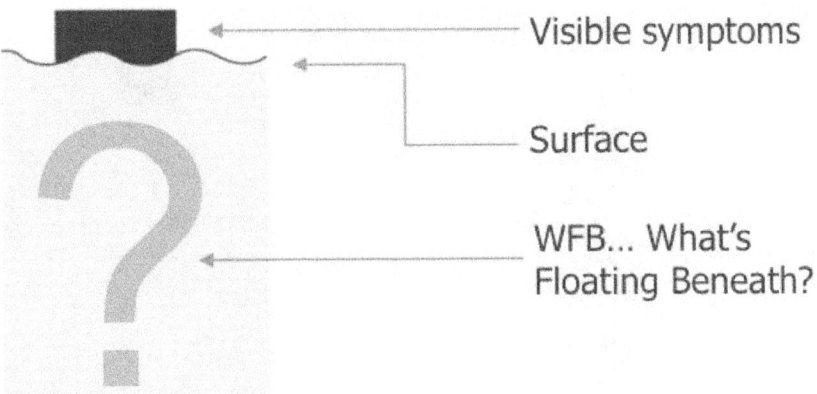

Figure 10: Visible Symptoms vs. WFB

Traditional managers often keep themselves busy without giving more than a cursory thought to the root cause of those symptoms. Root Cause Analysis is the only method to systematically eliminate the legacy problems that plague an organization and limit its productivity and success.

According to David Mann in his book *Creating a Lean Culture*, a root cause is "the basic source from which a problem grows, as distinct from symptoms that are the visible effects of a problem."

He further states: "By doing a problem solving analysis to find what is causing a problem, it is often possible to eliminate the cause altogether, or to prevent it from recurring." He continues: "By analogy, if you cut the top off a weed, it is likely to grow back from the undisturbed root. If you dig the weed out by the root, it will not come back."

The Business Dictionary website defines Root Cause Analysis as the "identification and evaluation of the reason for non-conformance, an undesirable condition, or a problem which (when solved) restores the status quo."

As such, Root Cause Analysis must be a system of logical thought that looks beyond the symptoms of an issue and discovers the underlying problem or situation causing inefficiency and challenge. Root Cause Analysis is a systematic approach predicated on the belief that without identifying the behaviors, circumstances, or actions that created an issue and implementing appropriate change at that level, common problems will continue to recur indefinitely (see slide below).

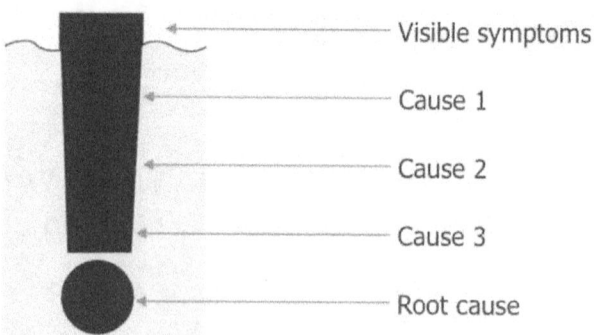

Figure 11: Visible Symptoms vs. Root Cause

Hold on, stop! Root Cause Thinking takes a lot of work! Does that mean I have to use Root Cause Thinking all the time? And when do I not use it?

Here are a few simple rules of thumb.

Use Root Cause Analysis in three situations: when simple events repeat themselves, related events happen regularly, or high impact events occur. Don't use it when issues are isolated, unrelated, or of low consequence.

But, don't fool yourself. I would argue that there are more reasons to apply at least a little Root Cause Thinking in most teams, so don't make up excuses not to do it. It may feel like going to the dentist at first, but the discipline will put you head and shoulders above many others in team effectiveness.

Here's the crux of it: Root Cause Thinking allows you to get things resolved.

So: what do you do? Gather a team when solving a problem. For Root Cause Analysis to be successful, you must consider the viewpoint of each stakeholder of the process. For example, manufacturing issues don't just impact manufacturing. Representatives from sales and marketing, administration, and logistics are also affected and may have valuable insight. Engage them in the problem-solving process. Failure to look at a problem from an entire system perspective can cloud your thinking and lower the effectiveness of your solution.

Have a look at Figure 12 on the next page. Have you seen this picture by Salvadore Dali? How many of the faces can you find? This highlights the point that problems are typically wrapped in traditional assumptions based on what you can and can't see. As you investigate a problem, you will more than likely come up against data that challenges your own assumptions and those of the team. Be willing to open your team to exploring possibilities you haven't previously considered. Without some elements of a free approach to a problem, you will have difficulty finding lasting, quality solutions.

Figure 12: Salvadore Dali's Hidden Faces

Since we're on the topic of illusions, over the page is a little detour to see second one from *Eyetricks*, a good book to buy.

Figure 13: A Face In Paris (From Eyetricks)

Figure 14, on page 50, shows a third amazing illusion called "Playing With Cars" from Francesco Mugnai's blog: (http://blogof.francescomugnai.com/).

Figure 14: Francesco Mugnai's "Playing With Cars"

And here's a fourth final one, just for overkill, before we proceed with "real work" (By Vurdlak at http://www.moillusions.com):

Figure 15: Vurdlak's Cow Illusion

Anyway, remember: look past the illusions to find reality and thus lasting solutions.

Shigeo Shingo, one of the world's leading experts on the Toyota Production System, said, "A relentless barrage of 'whys' is the best way to prepare your mind to pierce the clouded veil of thinking caused by the status quo. Use it often." He was speaking of the need to question every assumption by questioning the reasons for it. We will explore the Five Whys further in the next section.

Each member of your team comes to the problem with unique assumptions based on their experiences and perspectives. Challenge them to articulate those assumptions to the group by asking, "Why?" or, "How do we really know that?" as a point is raised.

Root Cause Analysis is based on the scientific method. It's very common to identify a root cause and propose and implement a solution. Don't just walk away at that point. A doctor checking symptoms and signs, then making a diagnosis, does not send you away without treatment. A solution is still a theory until its results are tested over time. Dedicate yourself and your team to long-run benefit and make sure to test results. Be willing to adjust the solution if needed.

Thorough analysis takes time. Make the time for analysis and investigation and be patient. While the initial investment of time might seem overwhelming, consider the cumulative time it takes to solve a legacy problem multiple times in a year. Suddenly, Root Cause Analysis can feel like a highly efficient process.

In this section, we shared the definition of what Root Cause Thinking is, how to clarify the difference between symptoms and roots, when you should use Root Cause Thinking, and how this can give you an edge in business.

***

Questions to consider:

What methods have you been using to get to your root cause?

Were you successful in defining it or did you find that the problem recurred over time?

Do you tend to target symptoms or do you dig deeper to the root causes?

When would be an appropriate time for you and your team to implement Root Cause Thinking?

7   SHOULD I APPLY JOURNALISTIC QUESTIONING?

"Who, what, and where, by what help, and by whose:

Why, how, and when, do many things disclose."

- Thomas Wilson

We're now going to look at what makes great journalists such excellent interrogators, fact-gatherers, and logisticians by discussing journalistic questioning and what it can do for you.

But first: a story for context.

You're a team leader working with a highly experienced new team member who joined three months ago. You've assigned him to write a report on the way forward in interacting with one of the company's key strategic partners. He hands in his 2-page report to you after a week of work. On review, you find that the report focuses mostly on the historical aspects of the relationship and does not address key issues of a proposed approach. Most of the material includes regurgitated points based only on team discussions. You're not sure how to help your team member, but you know that there should be a simple way to help him broaden his thinking.

In this section, we're going to define journalistic questioning, which is often referred to as the Kipling method, as well as discuss how to apply it day to day and how this can give your team the business edge you need.

Root Cause Analysis begins with clarifying the problem with the SMART Issues Approach and 6S Business Issues Clarification Model, but then further dissection is needed to flesh out the structure of the idea or issue being addressed. Usually business problems being dissected are complex and multifaceted (which is why they are lingering problems anyway) and therefore difficult to analyze.

Effective analysis is only possible when the scope of the problem is narrowed and clearly defined. The 5Ws and an H (or 2 Hs) method, shown in the slide below, is very useful for isolating a problem and defining it accurately. This quick approach uses the traditional "journalistic checklist" of asking what, who, where, when, why, along with how. This is done in the form of "means" and "ways;" in other words, looking at the resources available and circumstances around a historical problem or, alternately, questioning comprehensively around building a solution in the future.

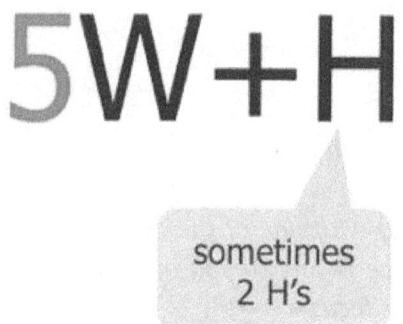

5W+H

sometimes
2 H's

- What happened?
- Who is involved?
- Where did it happen?
- When did it happen?
- Why did it happen?
- By what means?
- In what way? How?

Figure 16: Journalistic Questioning / 5W + H

These questions, or interrogative words, build a "complete report" of the factors surrounding a problem. To maximize the value of this method, questions should be as in depth as possible. They should not usually be closed yes/no types since their aim is to add value to a clear and concise problem statement that describes a specific issue in measurable, fact-based terms. Sounds simple, but despite being a common tool learned in early high school, most managers neglect using this nearly often or deliberately enough. Do you use it effectively?

Here's an example from a supply distribution business.

Let's say customers order ink cartridges for their printers via phone and Internet. In the past month, shipping errors have increased dramatically. Customers are complaining about receiving the wrong cartridges for their machines. It's clear that something must be done. A problem-solving team decides to deliberately use the 5Ws and 1H method to define and scope the problem as one simple dimension of attack.

What happened? Understanding the problem: In the past 30 days, 27% of ink cartridge orders were filled incorrectly. Seventy-five percent of the incorrect orders involved the same two part numbers.

Who is involved? The people involved: customers, warehouse staff, customer service representatives.

When did it happen? Duration of the problem: This problem occurred in 2% of orders shipped previous to the past 30 days. Frequency of shipping errors increased dramatically in the past 30 days.

Where did it happen? Location of the problem: This issue only occurs for orders shipped from Warehouse #3.

Why is it a problem? Justification for problem-solving: this issue negatively impacts customer satisfaction. Costs to ship replacement ink cartridges and stock returns are significant. Administrative costs are incurred to correct billing issues and repair customer relationships.

How do we resolve it? Problem-solving plan: due to the urgency of this issue, all shipments from warehouse #3 will be audited for accuracy to minimize customer complaints. A problem-solving team will conduct impact and Root Cause Analysis to identify causes and correct them.

By using the 5Ws and 1H method, the group has moved the issue from a vague understanding to a defined problem and a plan of action. A problem-solving team can now be created to investigate shipping errors from Warehouse #3 in the past 30 days. The investigation is focused on two part numbers and is justified by the threat to customer satisfaction and costs incurred if the problem is allowed to continue.

Using this method to define a problem creates a sense of urgency and ownership of the problem in the problem-solving team. It focuses the team on a measurable issue and directs their problem-solving efforts in the correct spirit.

Be careful, however, because 5Ws is not a form of very deep Root Cause Analysis. 5Ws forces the team to build a broad understanding of the context and lays the foundation for deeper structuring. The group can now move on to Root Cause Analysis to go deeper than 5Ws in various directions, but it still needs the journalistic mindset and "complete report checklist" mentality. We've looked at the problem broadly; it's now time to look at it more deeply.

In this section, we shared the definition of journalistic questioning and how to apply it for effective analysis.

***

Questions to consider:

What do you find most challenging when defining your root problem?

What past situations did you have where journalistic questioning could have been useful?

8   HOW CAN I DIG DEEPER WITH FIVE WHYS?

"Having no problems is the biggest problem of all... Ask 'why' five times about every matter."

- Taiichi Ohno

It's time to clarify a simple thinking tool that made the Toyota Production System famous: the Five Why process. This simple tool can do a lot for your solution. Even if you think you know how to use it, read on.

Here's a true story to consider.

You're sitting in a meeting with your team member in order to help them in a discussion with an irate potential key customer. The customer representative has been complaining about the quality of service in your company and wants you to act to help him. The team member you're sitting with loudly asks, "Why is this so?" The customer answers, and the team member again asks, "Why?" The customer is looking frustrated and asks back, "Why what?" The team member looks at you, unsure of how to proceed. You sense that, while your team member has been an enthusiastic interrogator and Five Whys fanatic, he's alienated the customer and not heard a word he's said.

In this section, we're going to share what the Five Whys thinking tool is, how to use the "whys" in the smartest, most constructive way, practical examples of how to use it, and how this can give you a business edge.

But first, let's briefly delve deeper into the history of this tool to understand it better: Why, no pun intended, did Taiichi Ohno come up with this? It was a situation wherein desperate times call for desperate measures, or perhaps desperate times call for simple but effective measures (which tend to be useful in most situations). Ohno was Toyota's plant manager after World War II, in 1950. World War II had ravaged Japan, two atom bombs had decimated the population, there were no supply lines, Toyota had no cash, and it was operating in a small, poor market. These are all great reasons to formalize a great thinking tool. Enter the Five Whys!

There are several methods for conducting successful Root Cause Analysis. The Five Whys method is one of the easiest to train and implement. This method, created by Sakichi Toyoda as part of the Toyota Production System, is a questioning technique to explore the deeper cause and effect relationships that exist within a problem. Eventually, often by the fifth question, the root cause comes to light.

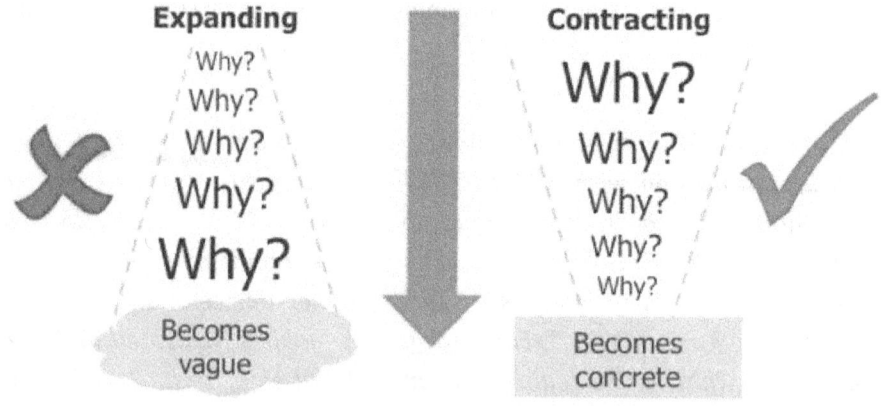

Figure 17: Two Types of Five Whys

Let's apply the Five Whys method to the problem raised in the previous section.

Customers who order Product A often receive Product B. (Problem)

Why? The wrong parts are picked for shipment.

Why? The employees have difficulty locating the correct part.

Why? The part numbers vary by only one digit and are often interchanged.

Why? The parts are stored next to each other in the warehouse.

Why? The storage bins are allocated by part size without considering part number similarity.

Why? The warehouse is at capacity creating space constraints.

Notice that the fifth why reveals a root cause of the current problem. The sixth why reveals a circumstance that is beyond the control of the process being analyzed. This example is simplistic, but it does reveal key points about the Five Whys system.

First, it's important to limit the scope of questioning to controllable issues. Failure to dig deeper into issues you can control leads to higher level, less tangible issues outside your influence. In this example, expanding warehouse capacity is outside the scope of influence for individuals involved in the shipping process. At best, they can make a recommendation for change, but can't see that change through to completion (but they should still try, of course!).

Second, a critical point to make is that it is possible to be too expansive in answering the Five Whys. Don't expand the problem to an uncontrollable point, for example: the world economy is depressed! Rather, "contract" problems towards addressable, controllable points. For example: my customer interaction.

Think about how to correct the root cause. Should we... label parts better? ... use bar codes for parts? ... separate the parts better? ... change make-up of storage bins mix? ... improve storage capacity? It may seem sufficient to move parts A and B to alternate locations and therefore correct the immediate problem. Will this prevent a recurring issue? Perhaps with these two parts, but other shipping errors are likely to occur. Correcting the root cause issue may require an analysis of space usage in the overall warehouse that considers part number similarity as well as size.

Let's do another clearer, but more telling, example that sounds a little like a Dr. Seuss book.

Here's a problem: I have a flat tire.

Why is the tire flat?

Because there is a nail in it.

Why is there a nail in it?

Because I ran over the nail on the floor.

Why was the nail on the floor?

Because it fell out of the box.

Why did it fall out of the box?

Because the box got wet in the rain.

Why did the box get wet in the rain?

Because there is a hole in the roof.

Wait a minute! So I just keep asking why brainlessly while my mind takes a rest? No. Try to avoid actually just asking why five times. It does not work very well. I've seen some enthusiastic team members get nowhere by peppering a teammate or colleague or expert with: why, why, why, why, why, why. It is important to ask the right questions, as well as the right people.

This is important: Despite great intentions, overzealous teams often just ask "why" too much! This interrupts thought processes, and paradoxically, quality insights then come less frequently. Release the constraints a little. Allow the team you're speaking with to answer the Five Whys more flexibly, more organically. Don't force it! Release the agenda and use the tool wisely. The initial fact-gathering process should involve extensive listening. Then, reapply the Five Whys retrospectively, or after the fact, based on the information you have gotten.

Let's continue by discussing countermeasures to the problem we raised above. Root cause issues rarely have a simple solution. Most often, eliminating a root cause issue requires a significant allocation of time and resources. Countermeasures are useful in the short term to allow time for addressing the root cause issue. In our example, a scheme of color-coding or additional employee training could reduce or eliminate shipping errors somewhat while the required space analysis is completed.

It's tempting to find a temporary countermeasure and implement it as a permanent solution to the current problem. This thinking is actually quite disruptive long term. Countermeasures give a false sense of security without eliminating the threat posed by a root cause problem.

We previously had the example of the shift workers being disciplined. Using the Five Whys questioning, this was the result:

Problem: productivity was flagging long before the end of shift, sometimes 30 minutes.

Why? Workers are trying to be first at the transport bus.

Why? Workers are trying to get to the changing rooms first.

Why? Workers are trying to get to the showers first.

Why? Workers are trying to have a quick shower before hot water runs out.

Why? Because a single water heater only accommodates half the shift. Such a problem was having <u>tens of thousands of dollars of impact per day</u>, while being solvable through a few thousand dollars of spending!

This is a really great example. However, there are limitations with the Five Whys system. It's possible to miss the root cause by asking surface-level questions or by focusing on symptoms without going to a deeper level.

In this section, we shared what the Five Whys thinking tool is, how to use the "whys" in the smartest, most constructive way, and a practical example of how to use it.

***

<u>Questions to consider:</u>

What are the most common pitfalls people make when using the Five Whys?

What other thinking tools do you think can deepen your understanding of a problem you're facing?

Is there an example of a countermeasure you have used? Did this work successfully or lead to long-term issues?

9 WHAT ARE THE MANY FACETS OF FISH BONES?

"Logic can often be reversed, but the effect does not precede the cause."

- Gregory Bateson

Having discussed the uni-dimensional Five Whys approach earlier, we're now going to discuss a multifaceted problem-structuring tool called the Fishbone Diagram and look at its relevance to multi-dimensional problems.

Let's take a look at a scenario for context.

Your team is debating the cause of a problem that has risen in your business's shipping department. Half the team believes that the problem has been caused by a software glitch, while the other half are certain that it was due to a staff scheduling problem. You offer that perhaps both aspects are important and both need to be investigated. An experienced engineer on the team speaks up with authority, saying, "A problem can only have a single root cause. That's pretty obvious from lean thinking."

That argument seems to make sense from an intuitive point of view. You've used the Five Whys quite often to arrive usually at a single root cause. But, could this approach be wrong?

In this section, we're going to share what Cause-Effect Diagrams (or Fishbone Diagrams) are, tips on how to use them effectively, why they are relevant day to day, and how this tool can give you a business edge.

To start, let's make some sense of what we know about Root Cause Analysis (RCA). There are two discrete dimensions of complexity that occur with most problems or opportunities that teams encounter.

First, how deeply do you solve the problem?

Second, are there one or more causes to the problem?

Unfortunately in today's environment, most teams, particularly in complex business environments, deal with multiple causes that also need to be "unpeeled," much like the proverbial onion. For this reason, there are actually three tools that need to be used together when structuring issues fully: 5W+H (discussed two sections ago), Five Whys (discussed in the previous section), and Fishbone Diagrams (discussed here).

So, what is a Fishbone? It's an effective next step in Root Cause Analysis through using a Fishbone Diagram (also called a Cause-Effect diagram or Ishikawa diagram). This is a visual representation of a problem and the causes that lead to it. While this is a useful individual problem-solving tool, it's even more powerful when used to stress a line of thinking in a group problem-solving session.

Fishbone Diagrams were apparently used extensively by Kaoru Ishikawa, the pioneer of quality management processes at the Kawasaki Shipyards in the 1950s and 1960s. Ishikawa went on to become a leader in both statistical process control and Root Cause Analysis.

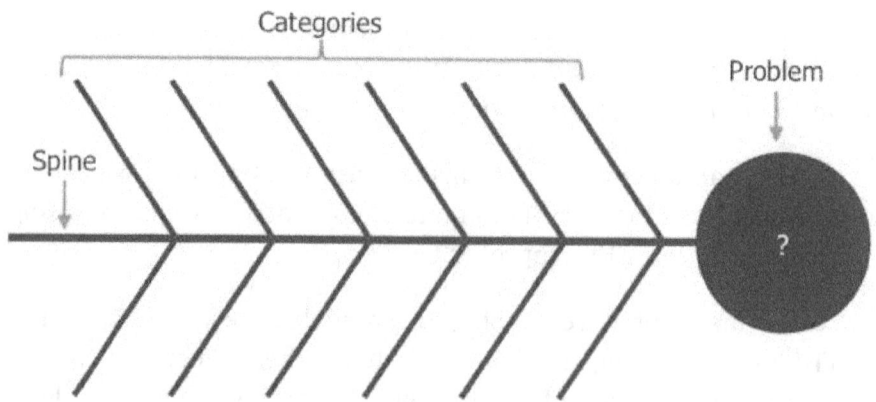

Figure 18: Fishbone Diagram Basics

As seen above, the Fishbone Diagram looks similar to the bones of a fish. The problem is traditionally identified in a circle on the far right. A long line is drawn towards the left, with shorter lines coming out from it toward the upper left and lower left, like a fish's bones. Traditionally, there are six lines to the top and six to the bottom, but this is not required. The key is to create one line off of the "spine" for each category of cause and label them.

There are many configurations of root cause categories. Here are a few standard ones. There is the family of P's, the M's and the S's (please excuse the implied abbreviation). Any of these, or none of these, can form the basis of the bones coming from the spine.

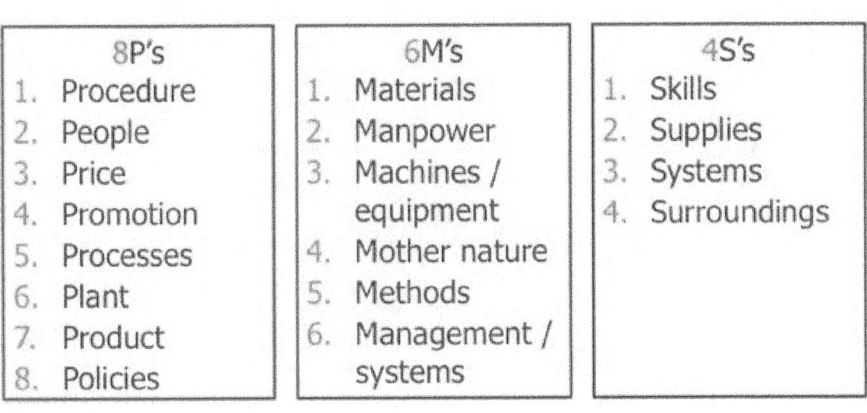

8P's	6M's	4S's
1. Procedure	1. Materials	1. Skills
2. People	2. Manpower	2. Supplies
3. Price	3. Machines /	3. Systems
4. Promotion	equipment	4. Surroundings
5. Processes	4. Mother nature	
6. Plant	5. Methods	
7. Product	6. Management /	
8. Policies	systems	

Figure 19: Fishbone Standard Configurations

For example, a service organization might choose to start out by grouping causes by Policies, Procedures, People, and Plant/Technology, and therefore require four lines. But this is completely up to the team. There should be no "rules," and of course, more specificity is better.

As questions are asked about the problem, possible causes are listed on the appropriate bone of the fish. It's important, as with other methods of Root Cause Analysis, to ask high quality questions that go beyond observable data but dig deeper (as per 5W+H a few sections earlier).

Validate any data presented by questioning its accuracy and determining how it has been or should be gathered. Look for hidden assumptions and reject them in favor of hard data[6]. For example, rather than assuming a procedure was followed, look for proven documentation of the procedure used and validate it, even if it's only a quick scan. It's amazing how many mythical unicorns and trolls many organizations or entire industries have.

As major causes are identified, it will be natural to ask why they occur or determine associated points to investigate. These issues are then listed in smaller "bones" coming off at an angle from the original. Here's a Fishbone Diagram of our previous section's example, around shipping errors.

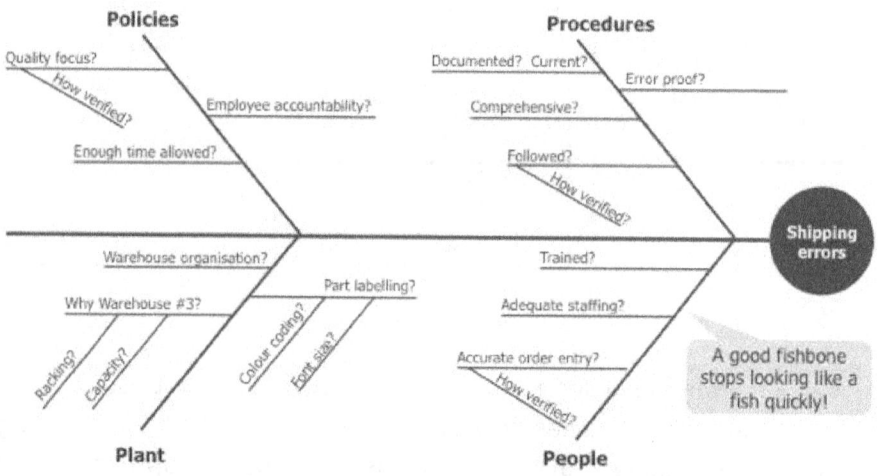

Figure 20: Fishbone Example

A Fishbone Diagram is very helpful when basic problem-structuring falls into a rut. Sometimes, the visual representation brings clarity and allows the group to consider alternative causes that were previously dismissed. Unlike the Five Whys method, a Fishbone Diagram

---

[6] This will be discussed in the second part of this series: "Solving Business Problems."

allows multiple causes to be considered in parallel, and should usually be used with more complex, longer-standing and non-operational matters.

While the Five Whys method by its nature only points to a single issue as the root cause, the Fishbone Diagram allows exploration of other contributing causes.

Let's go back to the example from the previous section: the ink cartridge shipment errors. Perhaps orders are inaccurate when taken or employees are not properly trained to distinguish between ink cartridges. It's possible that the procedures involved in the process are unclear or obsolete. It's even possible that the time allowed for processing orders is not adequate for good quality control. By raising each potential issue, the problem-solving team can view the issue from multiple angles, prioritize, and eliminate potential causes through corrective action.

As raised before, deeper, multifaceted problem-structuring is critical to more effective Root Cause Analysis. This is done through combining all three methods discussed previously, the 5W and H, the Five Whys, and the Fishbone Diagram. These combine well as three independent pieces, but also allude to the "king" of problem structuring (and "possibility" structuring), the Logic Tree. The Logic Tree will be discussed in the next few sections. Stay tuned!

In this section, we shared what Cause-Effect Diagrams, or Fishbone Diagrams, are, tips on how to use them effectively, and why they are relevant day to day.

***

Questions to consider:

Are there other tools you've used in getting to your root cause?

Did these tools prove themselves successful?

What challenges did you face using different approaches?

Are you open to the possibility of multiple root causes?

How could Fishbone Diagrams be successfully implemented into your problem-solving process?

10   WHAT IS THE ULTIMATE PROBLEM STRUCTURING TOOL?

"The logic of the world is prior to all truth and falsehood."

- Ludwig Wittgenstein

We're now going to clarify what we see as the "king" of problem structuring: the Logic Tree. This is a very flexible tool that can quickly make you more brilliant and insightful.

To start: a scenario for illustration.

You have asked for some brainstorming time in the team meeting. It's important for the team to decide what customer segments to target with the latest electronic gadget your company can offer. Here's a brainstormed list:

1. High-end consumers

2. Professionals, e. g. doctors, lawyers

3. Early adopters of technology

4. Individuals buying from our website

The team seems to like this list. You're not sure how to proceed, however, and are wondering how you can make sure you have not missed any other possibly vital audiences. The list seems strange, but you're not able to pinpoint your exact unhappiness with it. What do you do about this?

In this section, we're going to share what Logic Trees are good for, what standard trees look like, tips on how to use them effectively, and how they can give your team a strong business edge.

All problems have root causes, even if they may not be obvious. Typical problem structuring often starts with a "shotgun" approach, chasing every random lead imagined.

A more effective approach is more fact-based. This is about systematically gathering data, representing it graphically, and showing connections between the bits of information, often as a "Logic Tree." This branching structure enables teams to see where information is missing, what the potential cause-and-effect relationships are, and what the true root cause or expected future impacts might be.

Just like a real tree, a Logic Tree is made up of trunks and connected branches. With a living tree, you can follow the branches back to the roots; with a Logic Tree you can follow the branched effects of a problem back to one or more root causes.

Using these tools (not necessarily all of them), as well as the SMART Issues Approach to defining problems, determines that the right question is at your trunk, which we'll discuss further next. From this trunk, the tree has virtually unlimited branching opportunities and the branches can grow at any location along the trunk or branches. The branches of a real tree can sprout sub-branches; likewise, a Logic Tree's branches may include supporting questions or statements in sub-branches.

It's important to note before proceeding, however, that good teams don't just use Logic Trees and similar tools for getting to root causes, but rather also to explore opportunities, ideas, new possibilities, and future potential. Hence our initial push, in earlier sections, to use the SLOT Matrix to avoid fixating on urgent problems and to explore new possibilities as well as the positive and external factors.

So how do we do that through Logic Trees? Let's proceed to explore this further.

Firstly, remember the SMART Issues Approach we looked at a few sections ago? This said that we needed to remember the SMART aspects to clearly define and identify with specificity the key question we want to answer, or the statement we want to prove or disprove. This is the question or statement that becomes the trunk, or starting point, for our tree.

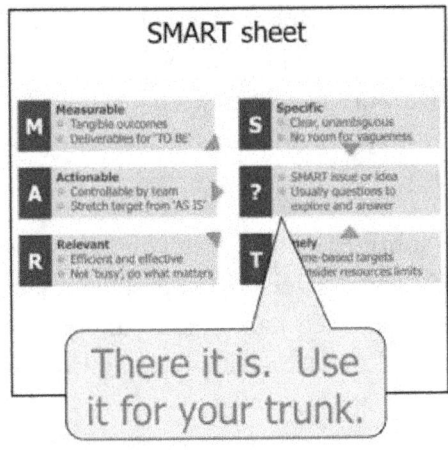

- Use the relevant SMART approach

- Take the question or statement defined

- Place this at the trunk of your logic tree

Figure 21: Logic Tree Trunks Come From Smart Sheets

Make sure to look at this in the context of the 6S Business Issues Clarification Model. Remember? These were setting, stakeholder, success, and so on, discussed earlier in this part of the Seven Smarter Team Successes series. From here, good questions or ideas branch out from the trunk into branches and sub-branches.

But how do we build a good Logic Tree? Here are some tips.

First, we must be aware of its "EEGO" (pronounced "ego"). You may have heard of the consulting term MECE before. This stands for Mutually Exclusive, Collectively Exhaustive. EEGO is this series' own, easier-to-use, way of saying and understanding something very similar.

EEGO says that a Logic Tree needs to obey three rules: (1) it needs to be Extensive, and then (2) Exclude Gaps, and lastly to (3) exclude Overlaps. Let's explain each of these in turn.

Extensive means to make sure you consider all possible answers to the question at the trunk. Don't prioritize or cut ideas initially. It's about having a full universe of possible answers to the question without judgment or exclusion.

Exclude Gaps means there should not be any possibilities missing between the branches of the tree. It's about trying to put a structure that covers all possibilities, even those you might not be considering consciously. It's often a lack of full awareness that causes us to miss key elements and creates gaps. A good Logic Tree avoids this relatively easily. We will give a practical example soon.

Exclude Overlaps is slightly subtler. This is about making sure that two or more branches do not both "cover" a lower level issue. Basically, don't have duplicates. A Logic Tree cannot be valid if two groups partially cover an issue. This makes further analysis ambiguous and difficult.

Please see the slide below for a clear view of EEGO.

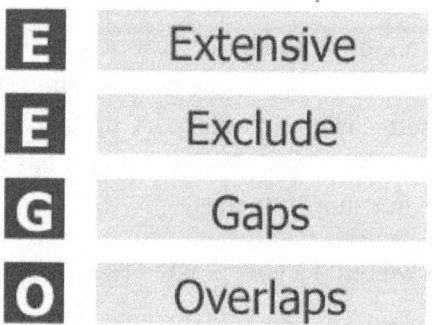

Figure 22: EEGO Acronym

Ambiguity can be detrimental for the problem structuring process. If the data is not extensive and has gaps, probable causes may be missed or wrong conclusions may be drawn. Excluding overlaps helps the problem-solving efforts to be more effective by keeping out redundancies that will drive wasted effort and inefficiencies.

Logic Trees are very useful.

First, their graphical representation is extremely helpful in problem structuring efforts. The old adage, "A picture is worth a thousand words," holds true here. In particular, the Logic Tree provides a visual representation of a tremendous amount of information with all the branching connections clearly shown. This is important to ensure that all participants in a problem structuring session are seeing the information clearly and applying similar interpretations of the situation. Imagine trying to be sure that multiple people understand, interpret, and use a chain of information the same way without a clear graphical representation. Information would quickly be lost or misunderstood and connections would be confusing. The Logic Tree provides clarity of a situation's information, while documenting complete understanding of known details.

Next, the tree provides groupings and separations that enable efficient and effective problem-solving and prioritization. The groupings enable teams to begin to see relationships and patterns that can provide specific insights, and they further allow quality problem-solving, which is explained at length in the next part of this series, "Solving Business Issues." Seeing information in related categories can help participants ensure that they have completed the "EEGO" parts of the analysis, having gathered extensive possibilities and excluded gaps and overlaps.

Likewise, separations allow participants to choose to focus on specific sections of the tree, knowing that all the requisite aspects are included in that bunching of branches. This ability to separate manageable chunks of information provides a welcome path for problem-solvers to follow a systematic thought process in individual sections. Teams can thus approach a problem in sequential steps, working on one grouping at a time, or they can assign these separate groups to multiple functional areas working simultaneously and stitching together at the interfaces. This is what allows the elephant to be eaten one bite at a time. Without the clarity of the Logic Tree, these groups would not maintain overall problem alignment efficiently.

Just as a real tree, the Logic Tree is a living creature. As new information is learned, the Logic Tree can be appended to incorporate new facts and observations. As this information is added in as branches and sub-branches, the overall effectiveness of the tree is tested and verified. If inconsistencies are encountered, the team can revisit the impacted grouping to ensure overall logic is maintained.

In this section, we shared what Logic Trees are good for, what standard trees look like, tips on how to use them effectively, and how they can give your team a strong business edge.

***

Questions to consider:

How often have you used a Logic Tree to get to the crux of a problem?

How do the different aspects of a Logic Tree make it an effective structuring tool?

Do you often consider "EEGO" in your analysis of business problems?

11 ARE THERE SHORTCUTS TO BUILDING GOOD LOGIC TREES?

"Reason means truth and those who are not governed by it take the chance that someday the sunken fact will rip the bottom out of their boat."

- Oliver Wendell Holmes Jr.

We started exploring Logic Trees in the previous section. Let us now dive into useful shortcuts to quickly build simple but useful Logic Trees.

Let's first explore a scenario for context, based on actual experience.

You are sitting with the CEO of your company. She's identified you as a high potential manager and wants to touch base with you. She's very interested in hearing your views on the company's latest forays into investment products. This is a far cry from your regular healthcare-related expertise and current portfolio. What can you say? How on earth can you sound insightful on an area of business you know very little about? You think about it for a moment, build a structure in your mind, and then share your views succinctly. Despite your inexperience in the sector, the CEO seems impressed with your considered approach. How is this possible?

In this section we're going to share the typical structure of Logic Trees, tips on how to use and construct them quickly, and why they are relevant day to day.

Before proceeding, make sure you're mindful of Oliver Wendell Holmes Jr.'s statement at the beginning of this section. Reason, with good structuring, is critical to avoid business surprises!

We've previously raised what Logic Trees look like, but how do you start one from scratch?

One of the first suggestions is to review the examples given and others to be sure that you can follow the what-how thinking process that is shown. There is a certain amount of spatial dexterity required in using this kind of a graphical representation. If you're not experienced with it, some ongoing practice in seeing and interpreting trees that are already out there will be helpful. You may be surprised at how quickly this tool grows on you if you use it a few times.

Various thinking tricks and frameworks can be helpful in creating Logic Trees. In a group setting, Logic Trees can best be created using large format chart paper and sticky notes. A large sheet of chart paper provides plenty of room to expand trees in whatever direction is needed. Sticky notes provide the ability to post information in brainstorm fashion, as initial problems structuring debates will suggest, and then shift each piece in location and interconnections as understanding is clarified. Facilitated brainstorming can be used to draw out information exhaustively and sort it to meet EEGO rules, as raised in the previous section. More on smarter brainstorming is available in the "Solving Business Issues" part of this series.

Unfortunately, electronic tools are often not ideal for the <u>initial</u> creation of Logic Trees. This is primarily because of the difficulty of seeing the whole tree at the same time during ideation. This is often a messy process in the land of large whiteboards, paper, and flipcharts.

Software-based tools can be useful for providing lasting documents of completed trees that can be retained and shared beyond group participants. Visio has a variety of templates with "snap-to" formatted drawing capabilities for charting that can be adapted to Logic Trees. Other specialized software programs specifically for Logic Trees of different types are available at reasonable rates, but a PowerPoint slide with a few boxes and lines can do the trick. Be sure to find an easy-to-use template so that inordinate time isn't spent trying to make the output "look pretty" (which clearly is not the best value you can add).

One mixed blessing of a Logic Tree relates to how it is used. Because it is clearly articulated and documented on paper, participants may see it as being etched in stone. That is far from the truth. Recall that, just like any living tree, a Logic Tree should grow and change as new information is discovered. While team members work and brainstorm, they must ask bold questions to challenge any items that might have been posted as assumptions rather than fact. These anomalies may become obvious when the flow doesn't seem to be correct. Participants will also be encouraged to ask bold questions in using the trees to predict future results. Asking expansive "what if" questions will help the team use the tree to follow logic to its probable end if one or more elements of the tree is changed.

So, how do you start from scratch if you have very limited context or inspiration?

First, one approach to building a strategic Logic Tree is to use traditional binary thinking. With this approach, an element is mapped to its opposite number or complementary component. For example, a tree might contain the financial impacts, mapped against... non-financial impacts. This logical path can then allow the non-financial path to be broken down further into branches like environmental or personnel, which you may not have thought of without this approach. This approach helps teams to look cross-functionally when doing problem-solving.

There are so many binaries that can be used: strategic vs. not, short vs. long term, current vs. future, existing vs. potential, etc.

Second, another approach is to look at a simple 2x2 matrix of binary dimensions mentioned above to map out key groups. As an example, this can use the same financial and non-financial elements just described above, overlaid with, say, a short-term and long-term view. It's useful to use the two most critical dimensions to map out these key groups, so carefully and thoughtfully list what these could be. As it turns out, there are often way too many options for dimensions. By using this approach, teams can focus in depth on specific areas to ensure that no critical details are overlooked and to include important considerations over time.

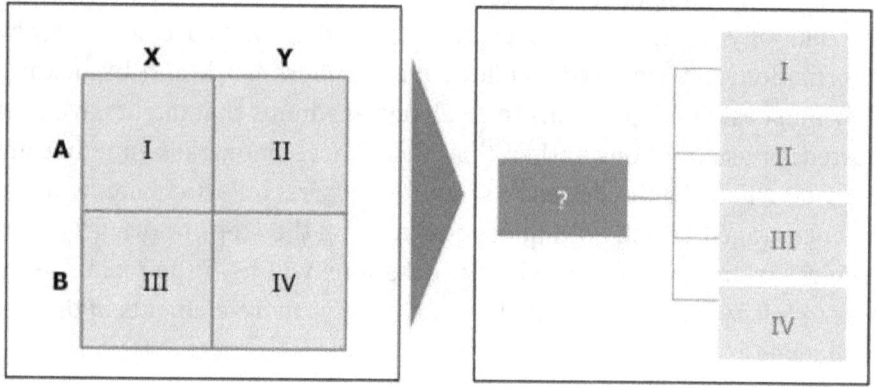

Figure 23: Matrix Structure Illustration

Third, questioning methodology can offer important groupings in creating Logic Trees. As always, closed questioning (yielding yes/no answers) adds little value for structuring, although it might for problem-solving, which we'll discuss in the next section. Open-ended questions to gather data will be most productive. The 5W+H Journalistic Questioning approach discussed earlier can also be used as branches in the Logic Tree. The answers to these will gather factual data to include on the trees as sub-branches or supporting points. Wherever participants don't know the answers to these questions, a placeholder can be created on the tree with an assignment to gather the missing information for future team problem-solving sessions.

Fourth, several business models exist for constructing strategic trees. First is Kenichi Ohmae's 3C model with Customers, Competitors, and Corporation (or Company) forming a strategic triangle, as discussed in an earlier section, relative to overlaying it against the SLOT Matrix. This model explores the overall business space. The team can then use a Venn diagram structure, comparing its own company in one circle to competitors in the other circle, to align with customer needs (for example). Of course, be wary of avoiding overlaps with this model and in using Venn diagrams.

Another business model is McKinsey's 7S model, also seen earlier, addressing the three hard elements of Strategy, Structure, and Systems, and the four soft elements of Shared Values, Skills, Style, and Staff. Articulating the elements in this interconnected heptagram helps to ensure an aligned view across a business. Recognizing that a change in one category can stress the overall system helps the team consider and plan changes in an integrated fashion.

Another model, known as PESTEL (Political, Economic, Social, Technological, Environmental, Legal) provides the prompts to capture critical external factors that can impact a business. This sometimes takes the shape of a wheel with hub and spokes, with the key business issue at the hub and contributing factors articulated in the six (or sometimes more) spokes.

All of these models have been mentioned before, and there are many other good ones (including, for example, the Seven Smarter Team Successes Model). Whatever business model is used, the general rule of thumb is to have three to six branches or groups to make a sensible, usable Logic Tree. Less than three may mean you are probably not pushing hard enough at the logical and creative thought processes to come up with options to fill all the possibilities and the gaps. More than six runs the risks of having confusion from too many details to assimilate; the groups are likely to start overlapping as well. Of course, these rules of thumb are just guidelines, not fixed and hard rules.

So let's use a simple example.

The key question will be placed at the trunk: How can I improve my profit?

A simple way to break this down is binary: income vs. expense. There is nothing else that makes up profit, so far as I know. Easy. The income can be from work, from investments, and from others. Expenses can be household, transport, and entertainment. Beyond this, take the tree 1 or 2 levels further, to X, Y, Z and beyond. There is no right answer, but this gives you an idea of how you could <u>use logic immediately after this section</u>.

Here's a more basic problem to demonstrate the EEGO rules. Let's say you had this key question: Where in the USA should I distribute new product X? You might brainstorm and say, Chicago, New York, and Los Angeles. What about the West Coast, East Coast, and Dallas?

Sounds silly in the context of Logic Trees, but teams often break quite a few EEGO rules unknowingly. Too much overlap, too many gaps. Let's rearrange it. Of course, this assumes that you're looking at the problem from the geographic perspective, which alludes to getting the 6S Business Issues context correct previously. Also, more on assumptions will be discussed in "Solve Business Problems."

A final point this raises is the importance of making sure the Logic Tree is consistent on one dimension, from trunk to sub-group, while also being relevant on others across sub-groups. <u>Consistency</u> means each level should deal with issues at roughly the same level of detail or granularity. <u>Relevance</u> is about making sure each sub-branch actually can address the trunk of the issues directly somehow. This allows the tree to be most useful to the team—remember: Garbage In, Garbage Out. If you choose to take anything specific from this section, consistency and relevance are probably the most important.

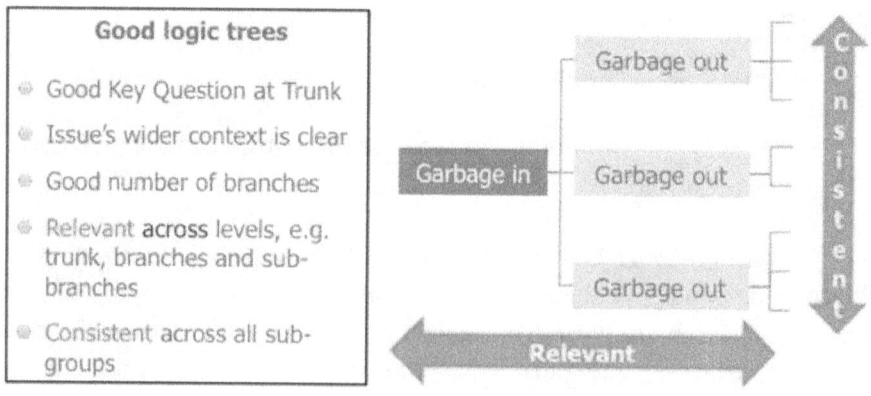

Figure 24: Good Logic Trees vs. GIGO

So here, we've taken the "king" of problem structuring, the Logic Tree, a little further and given practical structuring secrets. The concepts in this part are highly interconnected with the next part in the Seven Smarter Successes Series and will allow you to use this to move from problem structuring to problem-solving.

In this section, we shared what typical structure Logic Trees take, as well as tips on how to use and construct them quickly.

***

<u>Questions to consider:</u>

How do you normally breakdown problems to make them simpler and easier to tackle?

How have you seen Logic Trees started?

What are some external factors that impact your business?

How can you include binary factors to improve your problem-solving process?

12   DO LOGIC TREES HAVE DIFFERENT SHAPES AND SIZES?

"Logic, like whiskey, loses its beneficial effect when taken in too large quantities."

- Lord Dunsany

We're now going to take the traditional Logic Tree and give you a test drive of the different shapes it has and the issues it can address.

But first: a useful discovery.

Your team has recently discovered a simple but effective tool for problem structuring: the Logic Tree. Since using the trees, problem-solving has become more effective with the team using this simple tool to be more creative and specific in finding answers and levers that matter to the business. You've now used this a few times for individual work and have found it useful, but wonder what other situations it could be applied to. You've heard of Logic Trees being applied by individuals and teams to understand the current situation they are facing, the suggested way forward, and even to do team planning. It's time to find out more!

In this section, we're going to share what some more advanced Logic Trees are, tips on how to use them effectively, and how to group Logic Trees differently while identifying traps to avoid.

But first, please heed Lord Dunsany's caution given at the start of this section. We will encounter this warning later in this section.

There are many types of Logic Trees, which come in all shapes and sizes. In general, form follows function, so the shape of the Logic Tree will vary depending on the application. Some will literally look like a tree with a vertical trunk spreading into branches at the top and roots at the bottom, or more often left to right. Others may look like a wheel with central hub and spokes. Others may build to an amorphous shape. Simple projects may have just a handful of nodes or branches. Some complex projects may have hundreds of interconnected branches.

Logic Trees can be used for multiple functions. Teams may look at an issue and ask or answer questions to attempt to solve problems. Alternatively, they may provide statements of information to formulate hypotheses and plans of action.

A Logic Tree that asks questions is a type called an Issue Tree, since it gives issues, or rather questions, to be analyzed later. This breaks a question into further sub-questions. This is alluded to on the left side below. The Logic Tree that makes statements is called a Hypothesis Tree, giving potential answers. This gives statements to analyze later to be proved or disproved. Issue Trees are often more useful when an issue is more vague, often at the start of a problem process. On the other hand, a Hypothesis Tree is more useful when you have more industry, company, and functional context on the problem, as well as more data to support your assertions.

Simple difference: Issue Trees use critical questions; Hypothesis Trees use potential answers. Please see the slide below.

Issue trees ask questions	Hypothesis trees make statements
• Asks specific questions based on the structure of the problems	• States hypothesis and potential solutions / directions for action
• Gives questions to be answered with subsequent analysis	• Gives hypothesis to be analyzed to be proven or disproven
• Example: How can we increase sales by 10,000 units this quarter?	• Example: Targeting 30-35 age group will increase sales by 75%

Figure 25: Issue Trees vs. Hypothesis Trees

Up to now, we've only dealt with the typical, garden variety Logic Tree. However, many further concrete examples of Logic Trees are used in the Theory of Constraints (TOC), espoused by Eliahu Goldratt. Five different functions provide five different tree formats. Here's what we call them: Present Tree, Paradox Tree, Proposed Tree, Prerequisite Tree, and Planning Tree. Their conventional names, used by Goldratt, are given also. In actual use, the trees may include hundreds of elements. The types are given below.

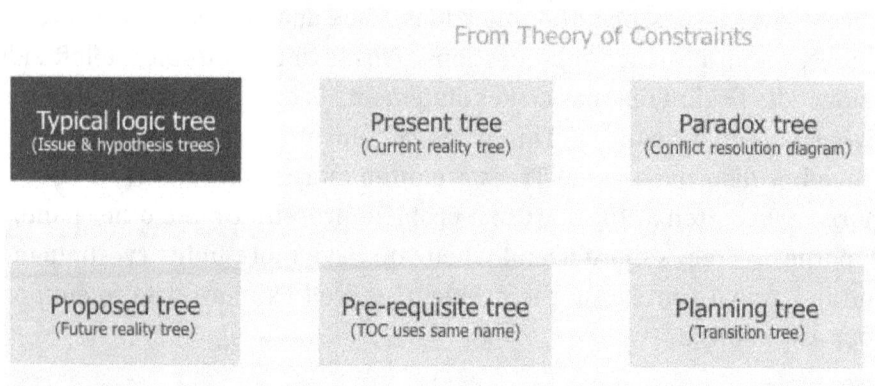

Figure 26: Typical vs. Advanced Logic Trees

First, the Present Tree, known as the TOC Current Reality Tree, captures all the current undesirable effects occurring in a system and ties them together to show cause-and-effect relationships. Connections and dependencies become clear so that participants can separate symptoms from true root causes. The Current Reality Tree below shows how the current reality for the undesirable effect of a car engine not starting can be traced back to the root cause of a clogged fuel line. Please see an example below.

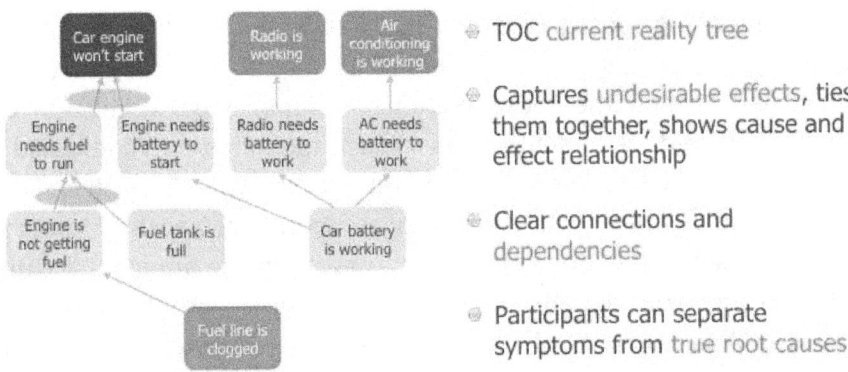

● TOC current reality tree

● Captures undesirable effects, ties them together, shows cause and effect relationship

● Clear connections and dependencies

● Participants can separate symptoms from true root causes

Figure 27: Present Tree

Second, the Paradox Tree, or a TOC Conflict Resolution Diagram (or evaporating cloud), can be very useful to help team members articulate their apparent conflicts and rework them so that the conflicts evaporate, helping the team members to identify and work toward a shared goal. This tree drives to win-win solutions. This sample shows how team members may start with mutually exclusive "must" requirements leading to ongoing conflict, antagonism, and reduced productivity. When the team focuses instead on the shared goal of being productive, they come up with a solution that enables both or all sides to have their true needs met while meeting the shared goal. See the example given below.

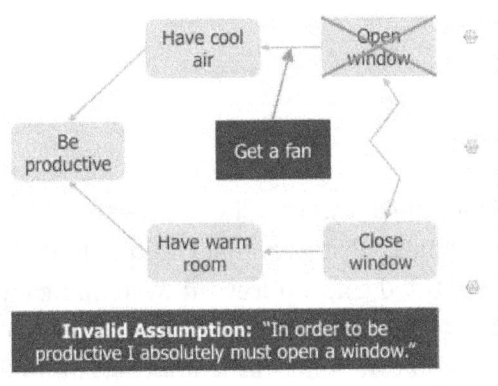

● TOC conflict resolution diagram / evaporating cloud

● Team members articulate conflicts and rework them to evaporate conflicts

● Identify and work toward a shared goal

Figure 28: Paradox Tree

Third, a Proposed Tree, or a TOC Future Reality Tree, is a natural build-on from the first two TOC trees. Once logical processes have been applied to develop the cause-and-effect relationships in the Current Reality Tree, and when conflicts have been identified and addressed in the evaporating cloud, the team can create a Proposed Tree that shows not only the desired results, but also any potential negative branches (also called a negative branching tree). These negative branches are then systematically trimmed to provide a clear best path forward. This Proposed Tree shows how a plan can be created using current reality information. Multiple future realities are identified when all current information is considered, including any negative branches. Please see the example shown below.

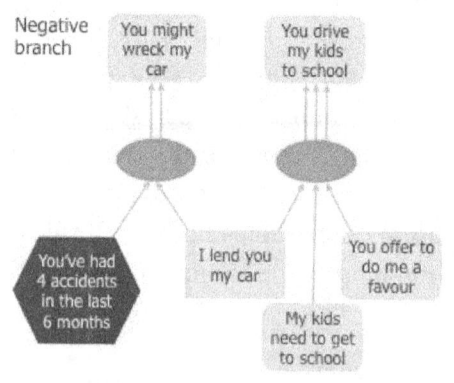

* TOC future reality tree

* Team creates a future reality tree that shows desired results and potential negative branches

* Branches are trimmed to provide clear best path forward

Figure 29: Proposed Tree

The Prerequisite Tree identifies intermediate objectives that must be achieved en route to final goals. Obstacles that could potentially prevent goal achievement are identified and addressed systematically. This approach helps a team to avoid counting on a plan that is focused on a solitary step for success, and instead can build in the appropriate time and resources to address a cascade of challenges pragmatically. An example is given over the page.

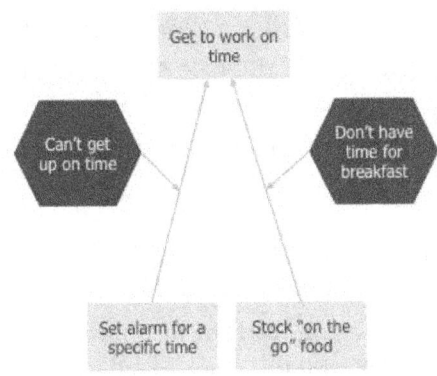

- Identifies intermediate objectives that must be achieves en route to final goals

- Potential obstacles are identified and addressed systematically

- Build in appropriate time and resources to address challenges

Figure 30: Prerequisite Tree

Fifth, the Planning Tree, otherwise known as a TOC Transition Tree, is used to outline a specific implementation plan. The team systematically identifies layers of needs, assumptions, and appropriate conditions, then defines actions. This continues stepwise until the ultimate goal is reached. Requiring the triad of needs, assumptions, and conditions is a method of mistake-proofing the process so that critical details are not overlooked. See an example shown below.

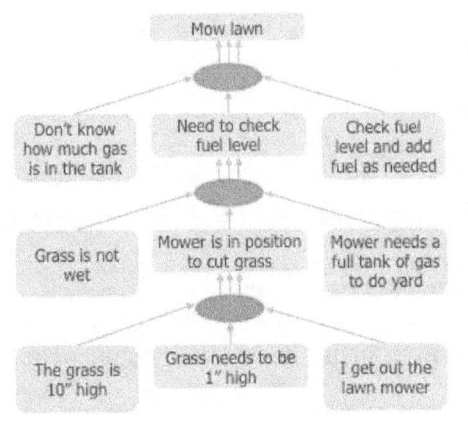

- TOC translation tree

- Can be used to outline a specific implementation plan

- Team identifies layers of needs, assumptions and appropriate conditions then defines actions

- This continues until goal is reached

Figure 31: Planning Tree

The substance behind all these trees is similar. First, the tree is intended to provide clarity and simplicity. Even these, though they look complex, can be used in everyday situations. Although a given tree may build several branches, each branch is a short sentence of facts or observations without extensive explanation. There is a consistency in the approach with all information on a given level of the tree demonstrating similar depth of the process. The tree can also be "read" upward and downward, signifying the "how" and "why" relationships between higher and lower branches.

Logic Trees allow for different arguments to be made. Clearly a logical flow can be followed from bottom to top or top to bottom. If the elements do not proceed logically, this is an indication of a flaw in the creation of that part of the Logic Tree. This logical flow can be used to explain the cause-and-effect relationships between the branches. Similarly, arguments can be made among the grouped branches. Looking at a defined section of the tree, the participant can see and articulate the EEGO rules in chunks.

In this section, we shared what some more advanced Logic Trees, tips on how to use them effectively, and how to group Logic Trees differently with traps to avoid. Make sure you use this information as is useful to you, but don't be rigid.

***

Questions to consider:

When would you use the advanced Logic Trees?

How do Logic Trees compare to using other Root Cause Tools such as Five Whys and Fishbones?

Are there any specialized Logic Trees that would benefit you and your team? How?

Do your Logic Trees proceed logically?

13   HOW DO LOGIC TREES BECOME ANALYSIS?

"The secret of success is to do the common things uncommonly well."

- John D. Rockefeller

Moving from theoretical problem-structuring to actual problem-solving, in the next part of the Seven Successes, is the bane of many managers. I don't know about you, but I've seen some well-structured strategies and theoretical groups of issues not move any further than just that. Once these teams structured their issues, they did not begin actual problem-solving.

In truth, many of the Structure and Solve tools are relatively intertwined, but the critical point is to move from ideas to evidence—and from there, to insights. The same way a doctor would understand the problem by taking a history, forming a hypothesis and differential diagnosis (and proposed treatment), then verifying this with appropriate examination and investigation.

For us to solve effectively in the next section, we need to know how to translate our structure into analysis. Whether you've used the Logic Tree or not, you likely have a list or groups of issues that need to be addressed. With a Logic Tree, these are the end nodes of your tree (all the smallest branches).

It's now time to debate this list of issues and delve deeper. In a previous section, we used EEGO to make sure that we were complete and left no gaps. We did this in order to make sure we were not missing "what we don't know we don't know." Now that we have the given collection of issues, it's time to prioritize (see chart below).

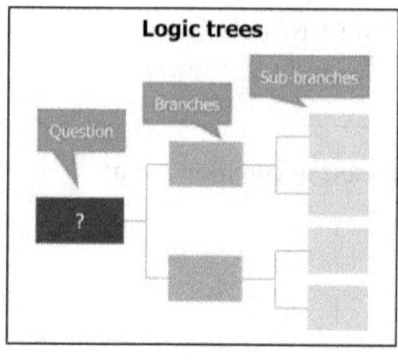

- Determine the most critical issues (through rough analysis)
- Balance bottom line and business health issues
- Once you've identified these, cut the rest off the tree or list
- You will end up with a list of branches / sub-branches to address
- These become your work packages

Figure 32: Logic Trees Muse Be Prioritized

Here is where back-of-the-envelope calculations of judgment calls come into play. Take a look at each of the issues on your Logic Tree and see if you think they are important. We will discuss Pareto Analysis separately later, but in essence, we need to get the most "bang for our buck"—in other words, the most critical issues to address, since you can't analyze them all. The challenge here is that not all issues have tangible impact, so make sure you balance your bottom line, business culture, and health issues when making your prioritization.

Some key questions to ask are:

What gives the biggest return?

What is the largest magnitude?

What lowers business risk the most?

What is quick to do?

What will have least resistance?

Once you've answered these questions and identified your priorities, cut the rest of the tree or list.

Here's a basic domestic example, that's "close to home."

Let's say you would like to renovate your home. You've identified the following areas to fix:

1. Expand front door and entranceway.

2. Make kitchen, dining room, and TV room open-planned.

3. Enclose patio and pool.

4. Build upper deck onto roof.

5. Increase three children's bedroom space.

6. Convert double carport to double garage.

After looking at the areas that would provide the most benefit, in this case in proportion to cost, you decide as a family that the following three are the most critical to do immediately:

1. Expand front door and entranceway,

2. Make kitchen, dining room, and TV room open-planned.

3. Increase three children's bedroom space.

This example gives you an idea of prioritizing the branches that are most important to you. You can now focus your effort mostly, or even entirely, on getting these three areas analyzed accurately. In such domestic cases, you've probably done a qualitative assessment of the benefit vs. the cost. In a business setting, you are much more likely to first assess the size of the impact (such as revenues or profit) and then compare it to cost. Some of these factors will be explored further when looking at the implementation matrix under "Suggest Business Solutions."

Now it's time to apply the Issues Analysis Flow, and its seven columns. This looks at each issue in turn, along with possible answers, supporting evidence, analysis needed, sources of data, and, ideally, who should do what by when (shown below).

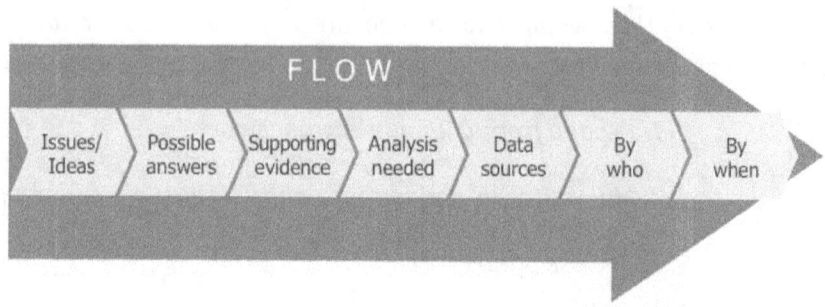

Figure 33: Issues Analysis Flow

Describe each issue clearly in a sentence. For example, one issue could be, stated as a question in this case, "Should we invest $5 million into Product X?"

Our possible answer is basically our hypothesis. We will discuss this idea more later, but the key message here is to put the best view on the table. For example: "Yes, we should invest in Product X, because our product mix is becoming limited."

Supporting evidence is about factors, facts, views, and opinions that you have picked up that support the possible answer. What are the assumptions you've made? Stating these makes it easier to conduct analysis further down the line. For example, a possible piece of evidence to support your hypothesis is: "Competitors are bringing out similar products and the profitability of the product is expected to be over 40% margin."

In order to move forward now, you require models and analyses that need to be done to verify or reject the possible answers. For example, this could be about doing a comparison of competitor products compared to Product X along various key dimensions, or forecasting the expected P and L for that product.

Finding reliable sources of data links back to sources in the 6S sheet and is simply about having using this structured approach to find the facts you need. In the example of the competitor analysis, perhaps there's a report that needs to be bought or a website to be visited to draw the features lists. This sounds simple, but not that many people actually do this deliberately enough.

Taking it further to understand who is doing the work and by when pushes this further into tangible business analysis and results in deliverables that can be tracked at a granular level periodically.

In order to do this, it's important to apply these aspects to all issues given. You already have the Logic Tree drawn; now you simply need to go through and apply the analysis. Once you've done this, it's important to dig deeper to understand exactly what problem-solving is and how to avoid its pitfalls. We will discuss this further in the next chapters.

In this chapter, we shared how a Logic Tree turns into analysis, pitfalls to avoid between structuring and solving, how to best conduct business analysis, and what this can do for your business edge. To take the analysis further please feel free to take advantage of the next part of the Seven Successes.

***

Questions to consider:

What steps have you been following to ensure you have usable analysis from the data you gathered from your Logic Tree?

What are your current business priorities?

What evidence supports the possible answers you have identified?

How will you distribute the pieces of problem-solving work among your team members?

REVIEW: TOOLS TO STRUCTURE BUSINESS ISSUES

"He who every morning plans the transaction of the day and follows out the plan, carries a thread that will guide him through the labyrinth of the most busy life."

- Victor Hugo

In this review section, we're going to recap all the material we discussed in the "Structure Business Issues" part of this Seven Successes Series. Remember, this is the first element of the Business Performance Chain, which makes up the first "half" of the Seven Smarter Team Successes Model. This review will be useful if you want to read a summary of this particular Success once in a while.

Wouldn't it be great to experience the following?

Let's say you're a new team member working on a fresh project. You jump in and start supporting the team's efforts. You are fitting in well with the team and delivering results. You're incredibly busy, but know you can handle the pressure of the work. The team notices your hard work and suggests that you present its findings at an update meeting with the new executive sponsor. You present to the executive sponsor, and he looks impressed. He asks you a few questions: What problem is the team addressing? Have you defined the issue? What are all the facets of the problem? You answer the questions with ease. Your team leader pulls you aside and says: Well done... but what's your secret to doing so well so quickly? You mention the Seven Smarter Team Successes to him and suggest that the team use it from now on.

In the first section, we discussed how to stop jumping to conclusions inappropriately. The SLOT Matrix shows the importance of stepping back on the causes limiting team or business performance. By looking at this collection of Strengths, Limitations, Opportunities, and Threats, you can SLOT test your objectives to make sure your view of your business team is complete. You can create your own SLOT matrix by overlaying other useful models on a "third" dimension.

We then moved on to using the SMART Issues Approach to business issues particularly in crisis and we looked at the importance of defining an issue clearly up front. SMART stands for Specific, Measurable, Actionable, Relevant, and Timely. We discussed how to create your own SMART Issues Approach by measuring each of its elements to support you in stepping back and defining your business issues.

We then looked deeper to find the importance of context-setting for business issues that you or your team face on a daily basis using the Business Issue Clarification Model of six factors. In order, these factors are: Setting, Stakeholders, Success (Defined), Scope (Clarified), Stoppers, and Sources. The aim of this model, also known as the 6S Sheet, is to start as an informal single-page anchor for the project or work package to be built up. Basically, it's taking the SMART issue or idea and looking at its context along six dimensions.

The next sections focused on Root Cause Thinking. It is important to get to the root cause and know What's Floating Beneath the surface. Root Cause Analysis is the only method to systematically eliminate the legacy problems that plague a team and limit its success. As part of this, we took a look at 5W+H, or Journalistic Questioning, in isolating a problem and defining it accurately.

We then dug deeper and looked at the advantages of using the Five Whys. To maximize the value of this method, questions should be as in depth as possible, not usually yes/no, with the aim of adding value to a clear and concise problem statement that describes a specific issue in measurable, fact-based terms. This helps in moving an issue from a vague understanding to a defined problem and a plan of action.

The Fishbone Diagram for Root Cause Analysis is a practical way of using the Five Whys thinking tool. It's a model that explores multiple cause-and-effect relationships that exist within a problem.

We then discussed the "king" of problem structuring tools, the Logic Tree. We looked at how to form the "trunk" of your tree. The trees branching structure enables teams to see where information is missing. Context is key for good trunks and branches within a Logic Tree. We introduced you to "EEGO," which says that a Logic Tree needs to obey three rules: it needs to be Extensive, and then Exclude Gaps, and lastly to exclude Overlaps.

We were then familiarized with tips to create Logic Trees easily from scratch. One approach to building a Logic Tree is to use binary thinking (remember, there are many more methods to help structure your problem). With this, an element is mapped to its opposite or complementary component, such as financial and non-financial points. We must also remember to realize the importance of making sure the Logic Tree is consistent on one dimension, from trunk to sub-group, while also being relevant on the others across sub-groups.

We have found these tools useful and hope you have too. We suggest you come back to this review section on a weekly or monthly basis to recap the tools and techniques. Spending just fifteen minutes a week reminding yourself of these or, better yet, bouncing them off others on a daily basis, can be incredibly valuable for your professional growth.

***

List of concepts, tools, and techniques in this part of the Seven Smarter Team Successes series:

1. SLOT Matrix

2. BCG Matrix

3. Ohmae's 3C Model

4. McKinsey's 7S Model

5. PESTEL Analysis

6. SMART Issues Approach/6S Sheet

7. Root Cause Analysis/Thinking

8. Journalistic Questioning/5W+H

9. Five Whys

10. Fishbone Diagrams/Cause-Effect Diagrams

11. Logic Trees

12. MECE/EEGO

13. Binary Thinking

14. Issue Trees

15. Hypothesis Trees

16. Present Tree

17. Paradox Tree

18. Proposed Tree

19. Pre-requisite Tree

20. Planning Tree

21. Logic Tree Prioritization

22. Issues Analysis Flow

So, What Can I Do Next?

"Life shrinks and expands in proportion to one's courage."

- Anaïs Nin

As a practicing medical doctor, I had many tricks and rules of thumb. For example, I always used an acronym called "JACCOL" when seeing patients. I learnt this in medical school and will never, for the rest of my life, forget what it stands for: Jaundice, Anemia, Clubbing, Cyanosis, Oedema, and Lymphadenopathy. They are embedded in my brain! Give them each a look if you are looking for something fun to do on a quiet Friday night!

When I first learnt this acronym I thought it was an interesting and catchy phrase, but didn't think much more of something so simple and so basic. Only years later, when rushing to see lines of patients at 3 AM and working 30-hour-straight shifts, did I really take in the value of simple tools. I also realized, however, that it had taken courage and effort to first apply them.

Simple tools are great to learn, and come in particularly handy when we need them most.

My sincere plea to you is this: Having read this material, please make use of it for your own benefit and that of your teams. Should it support you to be a fraction more efficient and effective in your work, and thus help you have more impact particularly in your professional life, then it has fulfilled its intended purpose!

You may wish to take advantage of the other elements in the Seven Successes of Smarter Teams series. In order, these include how to:

Structure Business Issues (this book)

Solve Business Problems

Simplify Business Messages

Suggest Business Solutions

Stimulate Team Motivation

Strengthen Team Capabilities

Support Team Alignment

Each of these seven elements provides a great menu of concepts, tools, and techniques to benefit from. Please feel free to use them and share them with your teams as widely as you wish.

BOOKS IN THIS SERIES

The titles and images below show you each part of the Seven Successes series for you to benefit from. You may wish to augment this book with any, or ideally all, of the parts below.

Part One: How to Structure Business Issues

(http://www.amazon.com/Seven-Successes-Smarter-Teams-ebook/dp/B00B4DL7O0)

Part Two: How to Solve Business Problems

(http://www.amazon.com/Seven-Successes-Smarter-Teams-ebook/dp/B00BUVLYJO)

Part Three: How to Simplify Business Messages

(http://www.amazon.com/Seven-Successes-Smarter-Teams-ebook/dp/B00CH67E40)

Part Four: How to Suggest Business Solutions

(http://www.amazon.com/Seven-Successes-Smarter-Teams-ebook/dp/B00CHPH1SA)

Part Five: How to Stimulate Team Motivation

(http://www.amazon.com/Seven-Successes-Smarter-Teams-ebook/dp/B00CLRWNNM)

Part Six: How to Strengthen Team Capabilities

(http://www.amazon.com/Seven-Successes-Smarter-Teams-ebook/dp/B00COROTH2)

Part Seven: How to Support Team Alignment

(http://www.amazon.com/Seven-Successes-Smarter-Teams-ebook/dp/B00D323I88)

BONUS MATERIAL ONLINE

Welcome! Take advantage of limited-time free access now: Take a quick 10-minute tour of the Seven Successes model right now! This talk was given at the Gordon Institute of Business Science in Sandton, South Africa. Please visit:

http://www.youtube.com/watch?v=uii0VEXig-Q

About The Author

Ali Matthew Monadjem, born in 1976 in Germany to a Persian physician father and an American teacher mother, is a medical doctor, management consultant, board member and social start-up addict. He grew up in the United States and Sub-Saharan Africa and graduated with a medical degree from the University of Cape Town in 2003. He worked as a rural and emergency response doctor and paramedic lecturer, after which he graduated in 2006 with an MBA, earning a Class Gold Medal for Distinction, from UCT's Graduate School of Business, an emerging market Financial Times Global Top 50 graduate school.

From 2007 to 2010, he worked with McKinsey & Company, first as an associate consultant and then as an engagement manager focused on strategy and organizational effectiveness. Here, he also aired a passion for knowledge-based empowerment by running ongoing recruiting and consultant training sessions, further giving lectures at various business schools.

He is a director at Accompany Advisory, a firm focused on business and leadership effectiveness. He also co-founded an emerging market mobile sector social enterprise and holds various start-up and public entity board advisory positions.

References

Ades, Dawn, ed. *Dali's Optical Illusions*. New Haven: Yale University Press, 2000.

Dettmer, William H. *Goldratt's Theory of Constraints: A Systems Approach to Continuous Improvement*. Milwaukee: ASQ Quality Press, 1997.

Doran, George T. "There's a S.M.A.R.T. way to write management's goals and objectives." *Management Review* 70.11. Nov. 1981: 35-36.

Drucker, Peter F. *The Practice of Management*. New York: HarperCollins Publishers, Inc., 1993.

Drucker, Peter F. *The Essential Drucker: The Best of Sixty Years of Peter Drucker's Essential Writings on Management*. New York: HarperCollins Publishers, Inc., 2008.

Kelleher, Kevin. *Cause-and-Effect Diagrams: Plain & Simple*. Madison: Joiner Associates Incorporated, 1995.

Kipling, Rudyard; Washington, Peter, ed. *Kipling: Poems*. New York: Random House, Inc., 2007.

Liker, Jeffrey. *The Toyota Way: 14 Management Principles from the World's Greatest Manufacturer*. New York: McGraw-Hill, 2004.

Ohmae, Kenichi. *The Mind of the Strategist: The Art of Japanese Business*. New York: McGraw-Hill, Inc., 1982.

Raia, Anthony P. "Goal setting and self-control." *Journal of Management Studies*, Vol. 2 Issue 1. Feb. 1965: 34-53.

Rasiel, Ethan. *The McKinsey Way*. New York: McGraw-Hill, 1999.

Rasiel, Ethan & Friga, Paul N. *The McKinsey Mind: Understanding and Implementing the Problem-Solving Tools and Management Techniques of the World's Top Strategic Consulting Firm.* New York: McGraw-Hill, 2001.

Sarcone, G. *Eyetricks.* London: Carlton Books Limited, 2007.

Stott, Phil. *Vault Guide to the Top 50 Management and Strategy Consulting Firms, 2013 Edition.* New York: Vault.com, Inc., 2013.

"Tandem." *Wikipedia.* 2012 <http://en.wikipedia.org/wiki/Tandem>.

Tennoe, Mariam T.; Henssonow, Susan F.; Surhone, Lambert M. *Base of the Pyramid.* Germany: Betascript Publishing, 2011.

Waterman, Robert H Jr. & Peters, Thomas J. *In Search of Excellence: Lessons from America's Best Run Companies.* New York: Warner Books, Inc., 1984.

Weiss, Antonia F. *Key Business Solutions: Essential problem-solving tools and techniques that every manager needs to know.* UK: Pearson Educated, Ltd., 2011.

www.ingramcontent.com/pod-product-compliance
Lightning Source LLC
Chambersburg PA
CBHW071230170526
45165CB00003B/1063